CW01506681

Haunted by
Past Lives

Haunted by Past Lives

A true story

SARAH TRUMAN

Sarah Truman © 2016

All rights reserved.

No parts of this publication may be reproduced, stored in a retrieval system, or transmitted in any form or by any means whatsoever without the prior permission of the publisher.

A record of this publication is available from the British Library.

ISBN 978-1-910027-13-4

Typesetting by Wordzworth Ltd
www.wordzworth.com

Cover design by Titanium Design Ltd
www.titaniumdesign.co.uk

Printed by Lightning Source UK
www.lightningsource.com

Cover image by Nigel Peace

Published by Local Legend
www.local-legend.co.uk

For Tom

I cherished, you perished, but darkness now surrenders to Light.
I shall never forget you, nor give up the fight.

Acknowledgements

I wish to give thanks for the patience and professionalism
of Nigel Peace, who has made this book possible.

About the Author & This Book

This is a true story. The author first met Tom Bailey in 1993 at a charity event and although he was rather older than her they became close friends and confidants. He was a determined and enthusiastic character with an unshakably positive mental attitude, known to his friends as 'Mr PMA'. A rugby player and speedway rider, with his feet on the ground, Tom also had a mystical side and mediumship abilities. In the thirteen years they spent together before his untimely death, Sarah's own spiritual interests and talents also developed. She is now a holistic therapist and Reiki healer.

While living "an ordinary, suburban life" together in Telford, Shropshire, one day Tom started talking about vivid dreams and visions he had experienced that seemed to describe a past aristocratic life in eighteenth century England. But, moreover, a deeply disturbing murder mystery was involved… The couple set out to investigate such 'facts' as Tom could remember. Their researches were remarkably thorough, blending psychic insights with hard academic work, detailed and professional, to the point where the truth of past lives seems to be the inevitable, simplest explanation.

Yet this was no dry and dusty research. As the quest developed, Sarah and Tom were unwittingly lifting the lid on dramatic supernatural phenomena that led to terrifying psychic attacks on the author.

This book is a tribute to Tom and, Sarah hopes, an inspiration to others on a spiritual journey to understand the true nature of being human.

Contents

1

The Mission

———

When Tom first told me that I had murdered him, I took no notice. We all know that dreams don't mean anything after all. It was 1994, the month of April had just begun and we were to find these dreams recurring for most of this month. Despite them being pretty vivid, I still dismissed them – after all, there was no way I was going to murder my closest friend! But he didn't dismiss them and at length neither could I, since I was prompted by a memorable dream myself in January of the following year. I'll write about this later. So in the February of 1995 I decided to play along with him and 'open up the case'. As it turned out, we discussed it often and quite unexpectedly the story unfolded in elaborate detail. What's more, I found that I could actually relate to some of it. Not wanting to miss anything, I began to take notes and soon became something of a sleuth in the process… Indeed, the itch to delve into this intriguing story grew even more.

I started by asking Tom if he knew when the murder happened. After giving it some thought he said it was roughly between 1740 and 1760, quickly adding with aplomb that it was during a visit to Tamworth Castle in Staffordshire. Confident of his convictions he went on to say that the murderer held a high position in society and that he was a young man, possibly in his early thirties. The victim was possibly around his late twenties and of smaller stature. Both were influential, although one was higher ranking; after some thought he said the latter was likely to have been the murderer.

In the same familiar manner, he continued that the pair were close friends from childhood and had much in common. The victim was a wayward sort, a Jack-the-lad, and this had appealed greatly to the murderer in their early days. Not wanting to sound clichéd, to hear him speak it was almost as if it had all happened yesterday. He was aware that the pair had originated from one of the southern counties, possibly around London, and that they had travelled widely around Britain together.

Strangely, at this point I had an inkling that they could have been related, although Tom refuted this. Out of curiosity, I found myself asking him if the murderer was married when he committed the crime – for some inexplicable reason I thought it might have some significance. It came as a surprise when Tom could tell me that he was and also that the victim was not. Strangely, even though I knew nothing about this story, I was vaguely aware that this point had relevance somehow and that a lot hinged upon it.

Did he know what the murderer looked like at all? It was a difficult question to answer under the alleged circumstances, but I felt I should ask since it was 'me'. Tom agreed awkwardly that he supposed he could be described as good-looking, although it's not really the sort of thing you notice when someone is about to kill you, is it? He had no recollection of his own appearance.

He then outlined the cause of the murder. Unfortunately, the culprit had believed a scandalous rumour that had in fact been a lie. It had been started by a young woman who was known to both men, and it appeared she'd had it in for them for quite some time. Tom described her as being of peasant stock, "an uneducated country wench". Nevertheless she was plainly the malevolent influence behind the deed, an evil character. (However, she met her nemesis later in life when she contracted a disease that caused her to die slowly and painfully.)

Following this, he revealed a slant to the story that I found quite insidious, saying that a good many people were jealous of the men's friendship. He didn't know why, but it was the key to what caused a lot of ill will towards the victim. This had festered for many years, starting from his childhood. Apparently all of this contributed to events leading up to the tragedy and also had a considerable effect thereafter. Jealousy is indeed a deadly poison and I could see that it could have been the root of the trouble. I really needed to know more, though. I held on, and there was more...

With regard to the scandal, Tom was aware that this too had been table talk for a long period of time, possibly for about a year. Things came to a head, however, when a lowly scullery maid uttered a comment that finally convinced the murderer to act. After saying this, Tom remarked that he was very surprised the murderer believed the rumour at all. But his reasoning was that if someone as simple as her knew about it, then it had to be true. Intrigued, I asked what the scandal was about, but Tom couldn't give any information at this time. In view of what came to light the following month, though, it was our general feeling that the victim had been accused of fathering the murderer's firstborn, although we were aware there were also other issues that remained obscure.

And now we come to the murder scene. It began with an assault which Tom believed took place in the kitchens at Tamworth Castle. He was aware of being alone with his murderer and that the air was heavy with hostility towards himself. He was shouted at and he retaliated. A fight broke out whereupon he was forced onto his back over a wooden table, used for putting the meat deliveries on. He recollects his assailant drawing his sword and inflicting injuries upon him, although at this point Tom's 'memory' became unclear about what actually happened. Despite the obscurity of this horrendous ordeal, however, he was vaguely aware of something happening to his hands and feet. Initially, he thought they were dismembered. I had my doubts about this, for reasons that follow.

He was aware of bleeding heavily around his guts, so reckons he received a death blow to that part of his body. What's more, his next coherent recall was standing spread-eagled against a wall in the castle dungeon with his limbs chained up, manacled and fettered. If this were so, I guess that he probably hadn't lost his hands and feet. I feel that he was aware of them being bound up tightly – nothing more that. He had no recollection of being put there. After giving it some thought, we concluded that the victim – Tom's former incarnation – must have drifted in and out of consciousness after the mutilation. He was left in this gruesome place for quite a long time, say twelve hours, as he was aware of the sun setting and rising again, after which he met his fate and bled to death.

Just suppose this is all true. Then it is no wonder, to me at least, that the pair would have had to come back to this world to atone for it all. But as I live and breathe, I can't see how this applies to me nowadays though! The story was drawn to a close when Tom mentioned that the scandal was disproved a short time after this tragic event, when another woman vouched for the victim's innocence. The murderer lived in bitter remorse for the rest of his life, which incidentally was a long time, especially considering the life expectancy of those days.

Tamworth Castle © the author

There was a memorable visit we made to Tamworth Castle just six months after Tom's visions began. I suddenly became unwell upon arriving there and as we drew closer to the place I felt nauseous, unlike anything I'd known before. I didn't suffer from any such illness, by the way. This awful feeling carried on throughout the whole tour, unfortunately, getting noticeably worse as I descended the stairs in the tower. I felt faint there. It came as a relief when the sickness began to wear off, but curiously this wasn't until we were on our way home. Later that day I saw a plan of the tower in an information booklet, and it was little surprise to see that the dungeon used to lie at the base of the tower. According to Tom, my reaction was because of the murderer's remorse after he had done the deed – especially when he later learned that his friend had been innocent.

Yet I have to say that I had a few queries about all of this. For instance, how could a murder happen at such a prominent place without some word of it leaking out, especially as they were only visitors? The fact that they were men of influence also raised an issue: weren't any enquiries made as to what had happened to the victim? Surely, especially if he held an influential position there'd be considerable measures taken to find out. Then again, life was rather different in those days. Getting away with such things was probably so much easier. I hoped that maybe in the fullness of time these questions would be answered.

Later this month we made another visit to 'the scene of the crime' to see what we could find out. After a seemingly fruitless expedition, Tom purchased an information pamphlet that outlined the castle's history. Bearing in mind Tom's belief that the pair of friends held influential positions, I made a note of the estate owners for that period. It seemed to me that if any direction for our investigation were to be found at all, it had to come from this source. For certain, I knew there was some ground work to be done here as neither of us knew anything about them.

We visited the main library at Telford to look up the relevant estate owners, namely the Townshends and the Comptons. We learned that George Townsend (1724–1807), Fourth Viscount and First Marquis, gained the estate from the Comptons, Fifth Earls of Northampton, in

1751. From then on it remained in his family until the latter part of the nineteenth century. Thus it became apparent how a murder could have taken place here and be kept under wraps, supposing the culprit had been connected with either of these honourable families. It did seem odd to be viewing them as suspects in what had now become a bizarre sleuthing game; although, from what I had read about nobility in days of yore, I supposed that anything could be possible…

I noticed that the above date fits in with the approximate time of 'the murder', but what I felt more relevant is that the estate was gained by marriage. Following my own intuition, did this place George Townshend at the top of the murder suspect list?

Corroborating our recent thoughts, the following month I noted two more points linking with Tom's story, this time concerning the murderer's age. In an account of the life of George Townshend in the Dictionary of National Biography, I read that his first child was born in 1755, which would have placed him at age thirty-one. There is also mention of him living into his eighties, which is undeniably a great age for that era. Did this longevity now become a conspicuous marker? Reading the account for himself, Tom also had an intuition that the Fourth Viscount Townshend was the culprit, although we both had to admit that the evidence was rather flimsy. It occurred to me that having seen what the murderer looked like in his vision, albeit vaguely, maybe he could identify him if he saw a picture of him. I say this because I had seen a reference to a full-length portrait of George Townshend by Joshua Reynolds that might give us an indication.

From reading the accounts I'd recently come upon, I was drawn to a few snippets about the life of the Fourth Viscount that somehow rang a bell with me. For instance, I noted that he was described by Lecky, a distinguished nineteenth century Irish historian and political theorist, as being "utterly destitute of tact and judgement." Apparently he could be rather rash at times, although I think arrogance had quite a bearing in this instance. I also felt oddly pleased to read at the end of the account that he was said to have been very handsome. I guessed that he might therefore have been very vain. I came to find out with time that this is an understatement – he absolutely adored himself to the point of having disregard for anyone else. I have to say that as I went through the motions of researching all this, my earlier scepticism began to shiver in light of my findings.

Later this same month we received copies of a few portraits of George Townshend from the National Portrait Gallery. Upon seeing one in particular, which was one of three half-length portraits by Mather Brown, Tom became convinced of the murderer's identity. This set of portraits was commissioned in 1796 to commemorate George becoming a Field Marshall, making him much older than the time of the alleged murder. But for Tom there was no mistaking him. The one that struck him most is memorable for the cold, ruthless expression. So, trusting Tom's judgement, we were both enthused by our discovery and believed we were starting to make progress. I do appreciate nevertheless that although we'd 'proved' this to ourselves, it probably wouldn't convince anyone else.

To summarise, it appears that the murder took place in what was by then the culprit's own estate around the time of the birth of his first child and heir apparent, which was April, 1755. This momentous event seems to be of increasing relevance to me in all of this. And we were soon able to identify another person connected with this saga, using the same methods we had used to find George...

I shall mention now that Tom had a spirit guide of whom he became aware soon after a near-death experience in 1961. It happened while he was working on the dam at Trewellyn in Wales. Late one night as he crossed a bridge on the site, he somehow lost his balance and fell from a height of fifteen feet, landing head first onto concrete. The injuries he sustained to his head were severe, as can be imagined, though he was very lucky; a large lump on the back of his head and a damaged nose were the only later reminders of the incident. Fortunately, the lump was well hidden by his hair and his nose looked okay. But unfortunately, he had lost all sense of smell. Whilst in hospital he 'died' temporarily and his spirit passed over to what he believed to be the astral plane. This visit was to be only brief, as it wasn't his time to pass over. Such experiences are common among those who have had NDEs, and there is considerable literature on the subject.

Soon after his recovery, Tom said, he became aware of the spirit of a woman who had stayed in contact ever since, as and when needed. In one of her initial messages, she confided that at some point in his life he would meet someone very significant to him, to whom he would give help, and that she would counsel him when the time came.

George, 4th Viscount and 1st Marquess Townshend
Gilbert Stuart c.1786
Courtesy of the Royal Ontario Museum

Tom and I first met in the late March of 1993 and became close friends in a short time. A couple of months later, and for the first time ever, he saw a full apparition of his spirit confidante during his sleep. He described her as being like a matriarch with a feisty, vivacious personality, who conveyed a hearty upper-class air. Her purpose was to advise him on a personal crises that I was facing at the time, and which I found strengthened the bond that was developing between us. Thereafter, Tom knew for certain that he had finally met the significant stranger to whom he was destined to give help in this life. Also, he knew that his own life was about to change.

Another time, he told me that his guide had not lived in this century, although he didn't know which. He was able to describe her appearance from the recent apparition, though, whereupon I distinguished her dress as that worn by eighteenth century aristocracy. He went on to say that although it is he who received messages from her, in actual fact she was closely linked with me and acted as my guide too. Indeed, at the beginning of our friendship her visits became quite frequent for a few months, occurring mainly in the early morning during Tom's sleep. I had never known anything like it before – it was most extraordinary! Was all of this really part of my fate?

So while reflecting on our recent discoveries about George Townshend – who, remember, was also an eighteenth century aristocrat – and considering Tom's assertion that I am a reincarnation of him, it occurred to me that our confidante might be related to me in some way. Could she have been George's mother, by any chance?

After receiving pictures of the Viscountess Townshend, nee Audrey Ethelreda Harrison, there was no doubt in Tom's mind as to whom he had seen, stating that she had appeared as rather older than the lady in the portraits. What a pivotal moment this was. Tom looked back over the three decades since his accident and reflected on the extraordinary acquaintance he now had with our celestial contact, who all that time had been just a presence in his subconscious. At this point, whatever scepticism I had disappeared since I could not doubt the authenticity of Tom's confidante and her influence in our lives at that time. It was awesome that soon after her one-time appearance we were able to link her with the first Marquis Townshend. It was like pieces of a jigsaw coming together. He told me that she had informed him that all would be revealed eventually.

It was my belief that we were on the brink of solving a most fascinating mystery. Yet I was left wondering something – why us?

Viscountess Audrey Ethelreda Townshend, nee Harrison
By John Faber the Younger
© The Fitzwilliam Museum, Cambridge

2

On the Trail of George

The penny drops

Now is a good time to mention the incident involving 'the drop-ping penny'. I appreciate that this may be open to interpretation, but I shall relate the story in full and leave others to form their own opinion. The incident occurred six months before Tom's momentous dreams began, so its meaning was a mystery to begin with. However, we came to look upon it as a significant marker later. The story began quite by chance as we had been working nearby Tamworth Castle; after finishing work we decided to treat ourselves to a tour around it. It was nothing more than a passing fancy of mine initially, a random trip down memory lane to my school days, but it turned out to be the first of quite a few visits we made thereafter.

It was a quiet Sunday afternoon in October, 1993. There were no other visitors about and a stillness hung over the whole building. During our solitary tour we came across an information board situated on the landing just outside 'the Haunted Bedroom'. I recall that we read about two ghosts known as the Black Lady and the White Lady who are said to have been sighted around the castle. I especially noted the latter, as it referred to St Editha, the ninth century foundress of Polesworth Abbey. Legend has it that around 1139 she appeared to the

11

Third Baron Marmion as he slept in this bedroom; she came through to warn him of the error of his ways concerning his maltreatment of the monks at her abbey.

As we read this we both thought of Tom's confidante, as we referred to her then, whereupon a one penny coin suddenly dropped from nowhere and landed on to the floor at our feet! It was uncanny, I actually saw it happen. On my left-hand side, just next to where I was standing, it dropped quite literally as if from out of thin air. It fell from a height of about two feet and landed with a resounding rattle. Tom was standing to my right and only became aware of it as it hit the floorboards.

Later, on our journey home, it occurred to me that the incident could be a pun on the well-known phrase. Tom agreed and also saw the implication, although he didn't know what it meant. So we were chilled by the thought and were left imagining all sorts of things. It was soon pushed to the back of our minds though, as nothing else happened until Tom had the dreams six months later.

I should mention that the last visit I had made there was on a school trip in the early seventies, so a few moons had passed. It was not a place that either of us had had much to do with in fact. I recall the school outing being pleasant enough with no spooky happenings as such. Indeed, there's not much I do remember in detail really, except for the guide telling us about the 'bailey'. Just the word has stuck, nothing else. By coincidence, this was Tom's surname. Also, the name Ethelflaeda left an impression on me, whereas it was the Lady of the Mercians who was being referred to then, not to be confused with our confidante Ethelreda. Do these shreds imply that my meeting Tom and the episode at Tamworth Castle were predestined? I believe so.

The Burial Place

In a similar vein, around this time I also recalled an incident that I believe connects with the burial place of our murder victim. It might again be a matter of opinion – indeed, far-fetched to those who don't experience such things – although for us there was no question about it as we experienced a vivid psychic insight while exploring the case that convinced us totally. Admittedly, it's unlikely there could be any tangible evidence as the alleged burial took place on heathland – otherwise termed 'wasteland' from a farming viewpoint and so-called because the soil is too acidic to cultivate. Under these conditions it is questionable whether there would be any skeletal remains given the time that has elapsed. Despite this, there is circumstantial evidence that gives food for thought, which I cover further on in this account.

Tom and I were journeying home from work one afternoon. It was sometime in late March of that year. The business we were involved with had drawn to an end that week and my mind turned to what had become my pet interest. Not expecting to find an answer, I asked myself where the body of the victim was buried… Suddenly, an image flashed into my mind from years ago that I immediately linked to Cannock Chase, a well-known beauty spot in south Staffordshire. I remembered an impression of a corpse's head that I had 'imagined' during an outing to this part. This had definitely been dredged up from deep in my memory's archives; I had forgotten all about it.

The year had been 1981 and I was approaching my seventeenth birthday. I was an Art student on a landscape study exercise and our party in a transit van parked on the car park at Milford Common. There was a feeling of excitement and everyone was keen to venture forth into the surrounding hills, so we all began to disperse to different areas that appealed to us. I wandered out towards Brocton, not realising that I had become quite separated from the others. Suddenly I became aware of being isolated and I turned to catch up with the safety of the group…

Panicking a little by this time, I climbed up a steep slope, uncomfortably aware of the strange, heavy stillness that was enveloping me. On reflection, it was similar to the atmosphere around Tamworth Castle on that later momentous Sunday afternoon. At this point I had an eerie feeling telling me that there was something untoward in connection with me, somehow, and I would see what it was if I looked behind me now. On so doing, I beheld the vivid impression of a human corpse near to where I was standing, so clear it looked real although I knew it wasn't. It reminded me of those zombie animations seen in films these days. The phrase 'like grim death' flickered through my thoughts and it was as if this was what it was hanging on for. Disturbingly, I could sense a close connection of some kind that had existed for a long time. It was almost as if this gruesome thing had been dogging me for many years, like a harbinger of bad luck. It made me shudder: was it meant to be me or someone else?

Upon reaching the safety of the group, I dismissed the experience as being a figment of my imagination. It was just the circumstances, wasn't it? The mind plays tricks in scary situations, so of course that's what it was. I'd never known anything like that before even so, nor since come to think of it. Returning to 1993, over the following days I realised that my next move was to persuade Tom to visit this part of Cannock Chase.

I shall return to this thread of the account further on. For now I move on to another very interesting finding that took place soon after, at a place called Arleston. Situated near to the old town of Wellington in Telford, which used to be an epicentre in days of yore, these parts are steeped in history dating back to the Middle Ages, so indeed it's quite possible that they could have some connection to our quest. The following account relates to a social contact, a close friendship even, that the Townshends had in this area of Shropshire. This is factual and is indeed compelling reading.

'The Gate Hangs Well' at Arleston

While out for an evening in this same month, quite by chance we came upon a three-star hotel called the Arleston Inn. Situated along a country lane leading to the old village of Arleston, this alluring place had only recently begun trading. Since Arleston was not a usual haunt of ours this was our first ever visit, although from the outset Tom felt that it had significance to our quest. Upon walking into the reception area, he picked up that 'a gate' and 'a well' had a bearing on it somehow, and felt sure there was something valuable dropped down this well. The owners told us that there actually is a well under the dining area and later showed us its whereabouts. Their company was cordial and they were interested when we told them about our quest. So we decided to make it our local.

One evening we booked the table that is positioned over the well, whereby Tom tried inducing a vision to find out what this was all about. This revealed abilities I didn't know he possessed and I watched closely as he went into what looked like a deep meditation for a few minutes. Upon his coming back, I was all agog to hear of the latest insights.

Firstly, he had a vision of a pendant with a gold crucifix attached to it, an exquisite item encrusted with an array of very expensive diamonds. He said it was given to George Townshend when actually his friend should have had it. After pausing for a while he added that it was a gift from a woman; maybe she was Roman Catholic, as he could see that the pendant was attached to a rosary. Next he saw George swaggering about wearing the pendant; there was an air of provocation as he teased his friend over his one-upmanship. In a sudden fit of temper, call it a 'paddy' if you like, the friend snatched it from George and stormed over to the well, where he dropped it down. Tom could sense the presence of an extremely deep well, possibly of unfathomed depth; there was no chance of the item's retrieval, although it didn't seem to matter to George at all. The cloud lifted and the two were soon reconciled.

As time went by, this turned out to be quite a relevant snippet since it was an indication of his former life upbringing. Notice the calling card of the rosary and the Roman Catholic woman especially. Apparently this scene had no connection with the murder, as Tom told me it happened about ten years before and on reflection it was only a tiff after all. It seemed as though the two men had a long association with these parts though and, from what we gathered, we thought they must have made regular visits here too.

To cut the story short regarding this lost treasure, we were to find that the incident didn't happen at Arleston Inn at all! No, it turned out to have been at the well in the keep of Tamworth Castle – surprising? Certainly there's proof that this one has the depth Tom spoke of and, after speaking with the man who renovated the land prior to the opening of Arleston Inn, we learned that the well there is shallow in comparison. By contrast, the well at the castle is so deep that the Curator told me they had to investigate it with cameras, as it is dangerous to venture down physically. Unfortunately, there's no chance of finding the pendant.

By way of an explanation for the confusion here, it seems that the energies were mixed up as Tom channelled them; this sometimes happens when mediums channel energy. In this case it was possibly because the incident at the castle happened around the same time that the men had visited Arleston, say, a week or so before. To confuse matters further, there's a well at both places. In fact, we found that this area of Telford is potholed with them. It seemed a likely explanation to us anyway. We concluded after that it would be best left for the visions to happen spontaneously, as they had before.

Cannock Chase

It especially took our interest to find that the counties of Staffordshire and Shropshire were connected by main roads which were part of a network of coaching routes in that era. Quite by chance, we came upon an antiquated map of Staffordshire dating back to the seventeenth century which clearly showed this. It explained the psychic sensations that I have always felt along some of these routes; I sense that George and his friend did a lot of gadding about, just as Tom had said at the beginning. So at last we were making some sense of this jumble. There's more information relating to Arleston that I have included further on, but for now I'll turn to the findings we made at Cannock Chase.

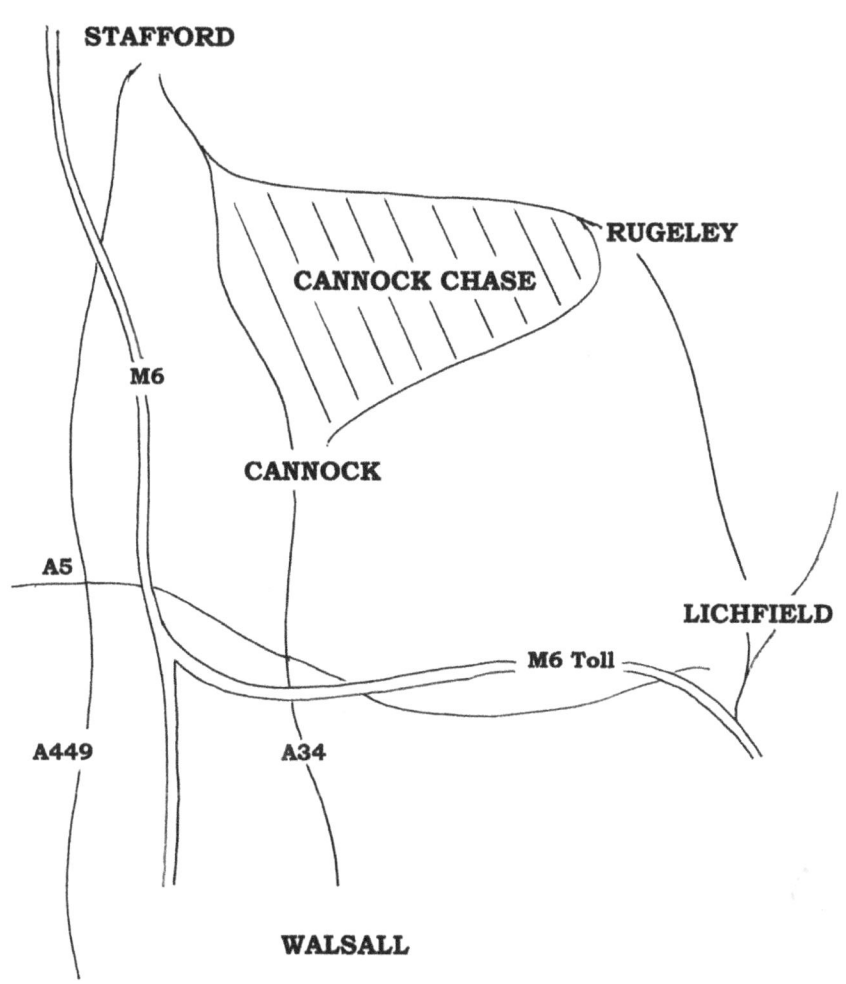

CANNOCK CHASE, STAFFORDSHIRE

I distinctly remember the 11th of March, as on this day I persuaded Tom to visit Cannock Chase to look for the burial ground, which seemed a better fish to fry than seeking the lost pendant. I was becoming more convinced about my insight, although for some reason Tom doubted it. After wandering around the general area I had covered all those years ago, we eventually came across a feature known as 'Oat Hill' which bore much significance. Actually it's prominently situated by the car park at Milford Common that I mentioned earlier. It took us only half an hour to find the burial spot, which wasn't bad going at all.

Upon reaching the summit of Oat Hill, Tom claimed to recognise the valley below saying that it had definite significance relating to the murder. After pondering on this for a while he noticed an old Norwegian Pine situated near the crown of the hill, although he didn't know why it drew him. It is the only one of its kind in those parts, perhaps suggesting that it is older than the other trees. It certainly looks like it. A few paces further on lies a copse of more recent pine trees, so Tom proceeded over there and upon walking over a spot among the cluster he suddenly felt a chill penetrate his whole being. In plain speak, it was like 'walking over one's own grave'. This was in stark contrast to the feeling of being hot and bothered, as he had been climbing the hill. More than content with our findings here, we therefore ended the search and set off home.

Later that evening I ruminated over the day's events in a hot bath, as you do. At the time, I thought that maybe it was something I had put in the water: as I lay soaking, a snippet of memory came back to me that I had forgotten all about. I now recollected walking past the copse at Oat Hill and a thrill of excitement suddenly fluttering through me as I glanced through the trees. There was no particular reason for it, so I now believe I was subconsciously aware of the significance of this place. I feel that deep down part of me knew I was about to have that macabre vision.

What is more, it also occurred to me that perhaps Townshend used the Norwegian Pine as a tether for his horse during the burial. It seemed likely, as I assume he was riding on horseback to this remote spot. Now, where did that come from? Who knows, but I can recommend an interlude in the bath as good therapy for anyone wanting to sort out the day's issues. I kept these insights to myself at the time as I didn't think anything much of them. But it turned out that they were quite lucid.

Around 8 a.m. of the 13th of March, Tom woke me with a beaming smile telling me that he had received confirmation of our findings. He had a visionary message in which he knew he was witnessing the burial of his own former incarnation. Once more he was able to give a clear account of what happened, which connects well with my insights.

He vividly saw a man he recognised as the Fourth Viscount Townshend approaching from the aforementioned valley beneath Oat Hill. He was on horseback, steadily progressing towards the incline of the hill. It was clear that there was something tied up in a sack flung over the front of the saddle; he knew that this was the corpse. Subsequently, he observed Townshend dismount at the foot of the hill and lead the horse to the top, whereupon he tethered it to a tree. By its overall appearance he recognised it as being the Norwegian Pine. He watched the culprit carry the body over to the burial spot a few paces further on; in contrast to the present-day, this was barren ground. He then set about the gruelling task of digging a shallow grave, the ground being hard and stony. Apparently it was springtime, as he had a recollection of the foliage being in bud. Could the month have been April, I wonder, when his eldest son George Ferrers was born?

Greatly enthused by these findings, a week or so afterwards we did some research on the history of Cannock Chase. We learned that parts of it were treacherous in those days: marshland floods had claimed a few lives. Perhaps this is why Townshend went to such lengths to choose the higher ground for a burial site? It particularly took our interest that George's grandfather, the salubrious 'Turnip Townshend', had once made attempts to cultivate parts of it. So it's very likely that his grandson was familiar with the region. We think there may have been connections here for generations. The nearest manor house is Shugborough Hall. I noted that the Anson family were the owners in that era, and since they were Members of Parliament it is very likely they were acquainted with the Townshends. The manor house is situated quite nearby to Milford Common, interestingly enough, so here at least is circumstantial evidence of our insights.

The same day I got access to a copy of Collins Peerage whereupon I gained another insight pertaining to His Lordship that took my notice: he was particularly generous in what he bequeathed to his daughters in his Last Will and Testament. I couldn't help feeling that this might have been inspired by guilt.

The Townshends of Raynham

On the 27th of April, 1995, we were to learn the true whereabouts of the Townshend family seat. At first we thought it was at Rainham in Essex, because of Tom's insight that they were from London. But in fact it was at Raynham in Norfolk. We found this out from Debrett's Peerage. We were relieved to find that it was still in a southern county, in any case, so we maintained our credibility about this. Moreover, we learned later that the Townshends also had a residence in Mayfair in London, which could also have a bearing on it all. Despite the fact that they were from Norfolk, I could swear that there's a stronger connection with London somehow.

Tom had another vision as he sat outside the Arleston Inn later this morning.

He claimed that he saw quite vividly what appeared to be three terraced cottages in place of the present-day building. He then saw his former incarnation taking his own and also his friend's horses into a stable nearby. They entered what he thought to be the left-hand cottage to settle down for a meal. For the first time, he saw his own appearance, although in very general terms. He was of short stature with long dark hair flowing onto his shoulders. He was seeing the men as they were at around the age of twenty, therefore it might relate to a time when the incident with the pendant happened.

So had the Arleston Inn been three cottages at one time? Well, maybe something like, as what was there originally remains obscure. At present there are houses that probably used to be nailers' cottages along Arleston Lane; this industry was flourishing for most of the eighteenth century, so I'll place a bet on that. The owners of the inn informed us that it had been a farmhouse earlier in the twentieth century and we were assured that this came from a reliable source. They also told us that during the 1950s it was turned into a public house, interestingly enough called 'The Gate Hangs Well', meaning that it was open and welcoming. Somehow this phrase had a definite resonance for Tom.

Of course, I just had to do some research into these findings and in the afternoon of May the 4th, 1995, I visited the Telford main library. Looking through the Local History section, I found a reference to a place called Arleston Manor, described as being tucked between the M54 and the old village. What's more, I was very interested to find that it is situated not far from the inn, about a quarter of a mile away in fact. The manor was described as having a fine timber frame, said to have been built as a royal hunting lodge during the 1600s. Enthused by the day's findings, I passed the news on to Tom and he agreed that it would be worth a visit. So two days later we drove to the site and sat outside on the driveway.

Arleston Manor as it is today
© the author

At that time the manor stood as a condemned building and everywhere was deserted upon our arrival. As it was described in the book, it is indeed tucked away into a corner of Arleston, although what stood before us was a shadow of what it was formerly. Tucked away and sadly forgotten about came to my mind as I surveyed the place; the grounds were overgrown and the house itself was in a very sorry state of repair.

After a while Tom began to receive familiar 'vibrations', which was always a good indication that we were onto something. We ventured through the wrought iron gate onto the lawn in front of the main door. It was here that Tom claimed to see us both, quite vividly, as young boys running in and out of this door, which he described rather intriguingly as being "always open". This had quite an impression on him. He said that the place had many happy memories relating to our former childhood days. He felt a close connection of some kind: perhaps the house had even been part of an estate of the Townshends'.

On reflection, was this in fact the significance of 'the gate that hangs well'? This certainly had a ring to it for us. It seems like the Townshends were made welcome at a few places around these parts.

One week later I again visited Telford library to find out more about the history of Arleston. Arleston Manor actually belonged to William Forester of Dothill, who died in 1758. He was an influential man of his day, becoming a Member of Parliament for Wenlock between 1714–1754. The manor was built at the same time as a wing was being added to the Old Hall at Wellington, which I noted with interest was also a Forester residence. As I read further, I found that the Old Hall had been passed down from generation to generation since the 1200s, thus making the Forester family well-established members of the landed society in Shropshire. I thought it worthwhile paying the Old Hall a visit.

To make the most of the day's visit, I decided to read up on some background about social and political events of that time. It felt like being back at school. Upon scanning through a volume of the Victorian History of Shropshire I noted how the Agricultural Revolution, which started in 1750, was 'a period of high summer' for the landed society.

Prominent landowners became very powerful during the reign of George III. The more influential among them controlled the county's representation in Parliament and had dealings in local government. They even went on to influence the affairs of larger boroughs. In particular, I noted that three of the largest estate owners local to this area of Shropshire were the Newports, the Leveson-Gowers and the Edgertons.

It raises questions as to whether there were connections between the Townshends of Raynham and any of the influential families living in Shropshire. Although the above findings seemed to disprove Tom's intuition about Arleston Manor being part of a Townshend estate, I still believed there was a link somewhere. It would certainly account for his recent visions, which strongly indicated this.

When I showed these findings to Tom later that day, he had a definite feeling there was some significance relating to Leveson-Gower, though he couldn't quite put his finger on it. He commented that there was a parallel relating to this present life, since in former years he had been acquainted with a member of this family's line. Although this may have a bearing on things, there was more that he couldn't define.

On the 24th of May we visited the Old Hall at Wellington, situated on the old A5 route to Shrewsbury. Nowadays this is a private school and in contrast to the manor at Arleston is a rather impressive sight to behold. We didn't venture inside, but upon walking through the grounds Tom became aware of a Duke of Wellington cedar tree which towers to a great height. He said he had recollections of us climbing it as young boys. The fork is about twelve feet from the ground and he could see himself throwing a rope up and knotting it.

So just what is the significance of Arleston? I can appreciate that readers might not see the wood for the trees right now! To summarise, we concluded that our coming upon this place was intended as a handle leading us to make all these rather important discoveries. For certain, the Townshends did have connections with this area of Shropshire, which you will discover further on, and I believe this is a foothold to some leading findings. Indeed, of all our insights Arleston transpired to give the most supporting evidence in fact.

The Salopian Townshends

In addition, another rather pertinent insight came to the fore. As it happened, this month was packed to the hilt with discoveries. In the last couple of days we visited a selection of public houses in north Shropshire and south Staffordshire that we thought could be linked with our quest. They had been coaching inns dating back to those times, and four in particular had familiar associations. Overall, it struck me that George and his friend did a lot of gallivanting in their time! I was to find that there's nothing surer: during one of these outings, Tom revealed that the duo were notorious for their womanising exploits, seducing many a comely lass they came upon, sometimes even taking them as mistresses.

For myself, I had an insight that George was incognito when he went about these exploits. I received a message from a guide one morning that conveyed how he masqueraded as a member of the working class on his visits to such places; this probably applied to his friend also so it seems that many of their conquests didn't even know whom they were fraternising with. My researches revealed that eighteenth century aristocracy generally were notorious for their promiscuity and the Townshends were no exception. Indeed, the duo's licentious exploits were amongst their most prominent traits, so maybe this has a bearing on why George was inclined to believe the fateful scandal about his friend.

In June, 1995, I went all out to find as much as possible about the landed society of Shropshire, doing a great deal of historical research. In the first instance, I was pleased to discover that there was indeed a Salopian branch of the Townshend family descended from Thomas of Mergate Hall, Braconash, Norfolk, dating back as far as the sixteenth century.[1] In the early 1600s I found mention of his descendant, Sir Henry Townshend of Cound, whose name I also found in connection with the areas of Cressage, Condover, Church Stretton and Ludlow in south Shropshire. This rang a bell, as I'd felt 'vibrations' in

---

[1] As complementary reading, I recommend The Lawless Coast by Neil Holmes. It puts flesh on the bones of the research I did in Norfolk.

all of these places in the past, Cound especially and this even before I met Tom.

I found mention of Sir Robert Townshend of Ludlow in south Shropshire, third son of Sir Roger Townshend of Raynham, Norfolk, and younger brother of John Townshend, an ancestor of the First Marquis Townshend. He died in 1581 and was buried in the chancel of Ludlow church. So here is an even earlier Shropshire link with the Townshends of Raynham. This is encouraging, but what follows next is even more thought-provoking: in the latter part of the eighteenth century I discovered that Anne Townshend, daughter of Robert Townshend, Barrister at Law, Recorder at Chester, married Cecil of Ross Hall, near Shrewsbury, the younger son of William Forester of Dothill.

Here indeed is definite evidence of an association between the Townshend and Forester families, albeit later than the period we were looking at. I was unable to find an earlier link, as the Townshends disappear from the Salopian records after the mid-1600s and reappear at Chester. There were no records in the Salopian pedigree either for Townshend/Forester marriages, so from this source we are left only with assumptions. Despite this though, the findings over the past couple of months strongly support our clairvoyant insights linking the Townshends with this area of Shropshire. Overall I believe I have made some leading discoveries here.

The next month, I was back on the case when I started looking into George's family background. I thought this would be a good place to find out who Tom had been formerly. Starting with his mother, I was interested to read that she became a Jacobite during the uprising of 1745, which is rather pertinent as it indicated the rocky relationship she had with her husband. It was all relevant to my purpose in the long run. Especially when we found out why their relationship was so rocky: George was placed in the family of the Duke of Cumberland during this time to remove him from her influence. So now we thought that maybe Tom had been connected with the Cumberland family... We put in a request for a search of books about the Duke, which became available to us the following month.

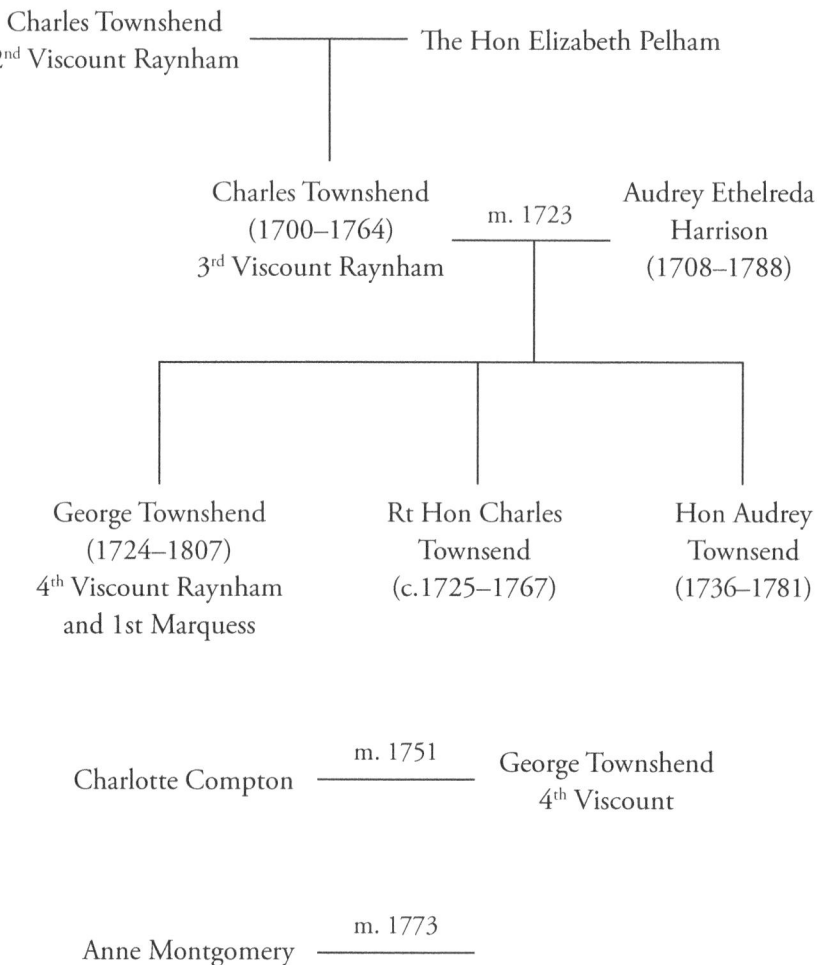

The Jacobite Uprising of 1745

In August we received an account of the Battle of Culloden called 'The Butcher and the Suppression of `45' by W A Speck. It is so titled because the Duke of Cumberland slaughtered the Jacobite rebels in that year once and for all. This tarnished his reputation so much that he was called 'the Butcher' thereafter. He was thought to be cruel and merciless towards the Highlanders, as their forces were no match for the English army.

From this source we deduced that Tom could not have been connected with this family, which surprisingly we found to be the royal family of the period. This in itself was enlightening. Tom was drawn to passages about the very influential parliamentary minister, Earl Granville. His hunch was clarified when we later linked Earl Granville with the Leveson-Gower family, from reading Burke's Peerage. It was another eureka moment: his name was John Carteret, the oldest surviving son of George, First Baron Carteret and his wife Lady Grace Granville.

Further, we learned that he was a very illustrious figure of his day. On his coming of age, he took his seat in the House of Lords and (sic) "for the rest of his life was never far from the centre of public life." Tom definitely felt that he had some connection with this man in his former incarnation, and intriguingly also believed that there is a significant link in this life too.

It has to be said that from Speck's account we gained some important insights about George when he served as a brigadier under the Duke's command. (sic) "He was not disposed to taking orders or tolerating methods of practice other than his own and therefore gave the Duke much provocation during the Suppression. Disagreements mounted to such a pitch that George retired from the military."

Upon seeing Townshend's caricatures of the Duke at that time, it became clear what was meant by "provocation" – it's a wonder he wasn't lynched. He was a pain to anyone in authority for that matter. As another example, he clashed with groups of local people during his governorship of Ireland, later in his career. An account in the Dictionary of National Biography tells about Townshend's opposition to the power of a knot of influential Irishmen called 'the Undertakers' and his corrupt attempts to break them, which were met with much scorn and which ultimately backfired. Because of this he became one of the most unpopular viceroys in Irish history. In one such episode, a group of these influential men published a series of powerful letters against him in the public press. These were subsequently collected into a small volume entitled 'Baratariana', memorable for a cartoon in the frontispiece depicting him with his tongue tied; underneath read the inscription 'And bid him to Hell, to Hell he goes'. These words in particular have a ring to them somehow as later I was to find that this had quite a pertinent bearing on what he might have had to atone for in a further incarnation. For Tom's part, after noting these points, he seems to have recollections of fighting in a battle too and of using a sword. That was his only comment. Perhaps, then, he had also been in the military at some stage. Maybe it was an attempt to emulate George, nothing more.

Following Tom's intuition about the Pelhams, we turned to reading about them next. The Pelham brothers were prominent parliamentary ministers during the suppression and were connected to the Townshends by marriage. However, as with the Duke, we could find nothing relevant to our objective and I thought it not worth pursuing. Tom still stuck to his guns even though he couldn't explain why. I suppose, considering that we had formerly known little or nothing about these historical figures, we were not doing too badly really. It's one step at a time in a lot of cases of research and patience is a virtue. Ours was to be well rewarded.

The private life of a Lord

We thought that researching into George's friends and colleagues could prove useful, therefore we decided the Townshend personal papers might provide some answers. On the 11th of October I phoned the Norwich Records Office, only to find that many of these documents were sold early this century and have been scattered all over the world. My informer told me with aplomb that the first Marquis Townshend was very famous and material relating to him was "much in demand from scholars and history enthusiasts".

But he suggested that there were two books which could be of help, namely R W Ketton-Cremer's 'The Phantom Duel' of 1956 and Sir C V F Townshend's 1901 'The Military Life of Field Marshall First Marquis George Townshend 1724–1807'. These contain information about George's life, referring to friends and associates in his military career. Incidentally, these were numerous as he was very popular and lived life to the full. My informer continued to elaborate on this, adding with roguish delight that George had at least three mistresses. I have to say that I found the latter remarks amusing when I first heard them, and it further impressed upon me that his licentious antics were amongst his most prominent traits. The Norwich records officer appeared to know much about the First Marquis Townshend pertaining to both his private and public lives. However, I drew a blank when I asked about one very close friend with whom George grew up. Such a pity.

The next day I put in a request for a search for the above titles. Strangely, in the days that followed, the remarks made about George's love life played on my mind; I had a hunch that it was one of those mistresses who was responsible for the terrible scandal... The more thought I gave it, the more familiar it seemed.

After thinking it over, I began to believe that the 'friend' in question just had to be a member of the Townshend family, having a connection with either parent. Since the pair grew up together, this seemed more than likely. More than ever, I was becoming convinced that Tom was wrong when he told me they were not related. My instinct also told me that George's mother was a key figure in this issue and I endeavoured to find out as much as possible about her. So on the 29th of November I wrote to the Norfolk Record Office, asking about literature on Audrey Ethelreda Harrison.

On the 9th of December I received a letter from the Norfolk Record Office telling me there was a book about Audrey, Lady Townshend, entitled 'The Lively Lady Townshend and her friends' by E Sherson and published in 1926. I was impressed to discover there had been a book written about her; she must have been quite a character and worthy of some coverage so perhaps this book would even give us some clues for our quest.

I picked up the long-awaited copy of 'The Phantom Duel' on the 2nd of January, 1996. Basically, it is an account of George behaving beneath himself in an episode concerning the Militia Bill he had organised in Norfolk. For certain, it showed that he could be rash and liable to over-react, so full of his own importance he was unreal.

The story tells of his annoyance with an elderly neighbour, who uttered a snide remark about his organisation of the Militia Bill. It's even comical, because the platoon was more like a Dads' Army! He found the old man's insolence intolerable and was so affronted in fact that he challenged him to a duel! This was totally inappropriate, since the old man was no match for him; George was aged thirty-five at the time and certainly would have killed him, had the event taken place, which luckily it didn't. The book states that George would have been found guilty of murder: does this sound familiar at all?

Skeletons in the cupboard

The other book recommended by the Norfolk Record Office arrived on the 2nd of February. The author refers mostly to George's military associations, although there are others. Overall it gives a much more favourable account of his character. Even so, later this month I did have a rather disquieting insight… But first things first, there are some thought-provoking findings I made this day that are worth including.

I was drawn to a section about George's personal life, in which he is said to have loved his first wife, Charlotte Compton, passionately. It appears that some aspects of his personal life always especially resonate with me. In particular, there were two rather touching letters George sent to Charlotte during the time that he was serving in Quebec, in which he earnestly declared his wish to return home to those who were dear to him. He came to realise that they had more importance than his career ambitions and he promised Charlotte that in the future he would seek the reverse of what fighting brings. When I first read this, I felt there was something relevant that was escaping me at the time; it later occurred to me that George had been neglectful of his nearest and dearest whilst in pursuit of his career, that he had rather taken them for granted.

In another section I noted that upon retiring from the military, after the discord with the Duke of Cumberland, he spent much of his time at Cramner Hall in Raynham. As it happens, this would have been around the time of the alleged murder. Perhaps this implies that the times he might have spent at Tamworth Castle were just visits; what's more, according to an information pamphlet about Tamworth Castle, it seems that he hardly spent any time there at all for that matter. Throughout his entire ownership, the place was neglected. Was this because it had bad associations for him?

I was drawn to a comment made by the author of the book about his prestigious ancestor, which I found rather impressive, (sic) "Townshend was possessed of great energy and determination when carrying out an enterprise; he was cool in action, and showed great abilities and qualifications for high command, and had the strictest sense of honour and duties of a gentleman." Yet it seems that he could also behave quite contrary to this. Since I'm reciting quotations here, I'll mention a favourite saying of Tom's while I'm at it: "There's nowt so queer as folk," as they say in Yorkshire. This seems fitting, especially as I know for certain that George was said to have been an eccentric!

Over the months of March and April in 1996, we made further attempts to find out who Tom had been previously. We tried looking through the archives of the public schools that George attended, but to no avail. Apparently, he didn't attend any other British schools either. Tom's idea then was to scan the lists of those who attended public schools in the said era to see if any of the names had a familiarity for him. On so doing, as ever, the name Leveson-Gower rang a bell for him and, interestingly enough, he also noticed Henry Pelham.

So we referred to the literature we had about the Pelhams from the year before and discovered that Henry Pelham and his brother had frequent exchanges with John Carteret, later Earl Granville. So it appears that Leveson-Gower and his associates have some significance to Tom's former identity. We gave our thanks to those who had kindly compiled the lists for us and considered our next move. (I'll describe later that I discovered he had been schooled in Dublin, but there are no material records of this. If my intuition is right, I don't believe he was an academic in any case and it's more likely he played truant a lot of the time. I was to find that there is a better chance of tracing people associated with him, rather than finding him.)

On the 9th of May I received a letter from the British Library confirming that they held a copy of 'The Lively Lady Townshend and her Friends'. Making a note of the publisher, I contacted them about obtaining a copy, whereupon I was told there were only two in existence. One was held at the British Library and the other was at the library of their subsidiary company based at Rushden, Northampton, but neither of them were available for lending. So we decided that we would pay a visit to this library in hope of a result. I firmly believed that this book held clues relevant to our quest and the journey would be worthwhile, so later this month we made arrangements to visit the publisher's library.

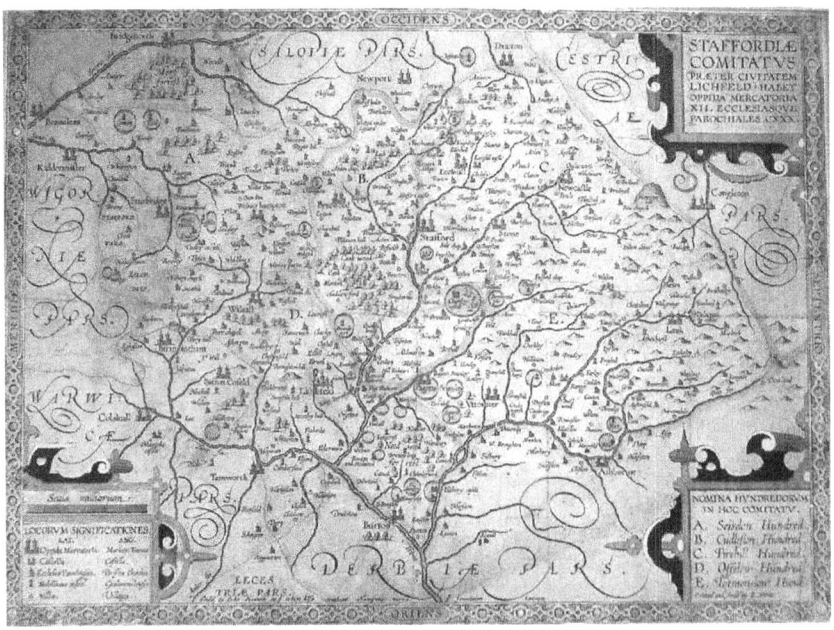

Antique map of Staffordshire 1602
Courtesy of Ordnance Survey

3

Where There's a Will

My brother, my lovely brother

Over the next three months another array of compelling discoveries came to light, some which again proved rather disquieting. I'll begin with our trip to Northampton on the 4th of June, 1996, and the findings we made there. Tom kept singing a song that morning while we were getting ready to leave, sounding like something from the old Music Hall era that I'd never heard him sing before. It was just the one line he sang, over and over: "My brother, my lovely brother…" On reflection, I think he must have been aware of what to look for in the book before we set off. From the way he flicked through the pages until he came upon the particular passages below, it does seem likely, as though he had something specific in mind.

Upon visiting Reed's library we were able to study the long sought-after book about Audrey, Lady Townshend; it proved thought-provoking and we scanned the pages with avid interest. There were just a couple of passages that drew Tom's attention especially, the first commenting on the Viscountess' husband, Charles: (sic) "[He] was an ungracious, surly individual cast in a very different mould to his lovely wife. There is no doubt that the curiously low tastes and eccentric doings of Lord Townshend led to her voluntary separation from him in 1741."

The other passage that held his interest was from 'Sorrows and The Last Years': (sic) "He died in 1764 leaving three children by a house-maid on the Raynham estate to whom he bequeathed £50,000. He left nothing to his brilliant son Charles (the Rt Hon Charles Townshend, 1725–1767), Chancellor of the Exchequer; to his widow only what was compelled by settlement; and to his son George what was entailed on the title. Whatsoever may have been the faults of my Lady Townshend, there can be no question as to the abominable treatment meted out to her and her children by this most selfish man."

Curiously, after scanning through the whole book, these passages were all that had significance for Tom; he had an inkling that he was one of these offspring and finding reference to the housemaid confirmed it. I still believe this to be right, although from findings made much later I concluded that there must be a crossed wire here as to which housemaid was his mother, as His Lordship had a few liaisons with servants. It appears to me that Tom's former-life mother had been involved with Charles at a time well before the mistress referred to in this passage, whom I learned to be a housekeeper by the name of Elizabeth Walker. It couldn't have been her because the dates don't fit, but unfortunately she's the only one on record. Also, a study of His Lordship's Last Will and Testament at length proves Sherson's figure of £50,000 to be wrong. Evidently, Sherson's accounts are not the most reliable source when it comes to facts and figures. Actually, I was to find this to be true of several points he mentions.[2] Nevertheless, His Lordship's draft wills did show a generous amount intended for Elizabeth, while later on he cut her out completely and favoured the children only.

It seemed to me that evidence of another mistress had also been cut out completely from all his household accounts: the records pre-1738

---

[2] It was interesting to learn that Erroll Sherson was in fact an ancestor of the current Townshends of Raynham, and his biography of Audrey Ethelreda Harrison seems to have been intended to set the record straight about the much-maligned character of his predecessor.

are missing in the Townshend papers. If he didn't do this, it was probably one of his descendants.

For my part, I gathered from other chapters in Sherson's book that jealousy and scandal-mongering appear to have plagued Audrey in her time. The book title describes her as "Lively" but I think 'flighty' would be the modern word that seems more appropriate. She was a spirited, vivacious type, and a lover of high society parties and the latest fashion trends. She was among the first to wear black stockings – very risqué! Although how anyone could notice under all those crinolines they used to wear is a puzzle, unless she lifted them up a lot… She was often seen on the arm of one of her escorts to these social events, which earned her much notoriety. I noticed that Casanova was among the guests at one such event; had she been seen on his arm by any chance? If so, it would explain why she was talked about.

In general, though, high society was really stuffy in that era. Actually it was her husband who was the unfaithful one with a string of conquests, so it is said. Luckily for her she was of independent means, as he often treated her badly for much of their marriage. In the circumstances, she might easily have hidden herself away, but instead she was doing the social rounds. The status of women in those days was unenviable and girls could be wed as young as twelve years of age, although I learned later that this was exceptional and on average women married around the age of twenty-four. But women over thirty were considered to be 'on the shelf' if still unmarried and indeed getting on a bit by their late twenties.

I was to discover later that Charles had in fact spurned Audrey at that time in her life for a teenaged mistress, whom I believe was Tom's former-life mother. As it happened, I got what can be described as a 'newsflash' in a vision one morning, clearly indicating this: I saw a maid serving meals to a couple whom I knew to be Lord and Lady Townshend. Clad in a revealing bodice that clearly displayed her ample bosom, there was an air of swagger about her as she placed the plates onto the dining table. Charles ogled her with relish as Lady Townshend forlornly looked on. How humiliating, a brazen serving wench was wiping the floor with the lady of the house, whose husband apparently regarded her as 'past it' by then.

Somehow it seems fitting that George Townshend's best friend from his childhood was in fact his half-brother, highly favoured considering that he was the base-born son of a serving wench. Tom suggested that this was because he was a love-child. It started to become clear why many were jealous of their friendship and also why George had the upper hand.

Our trip to the library had raised a whole host of new questions, but overall it had been well worthwhile and it appeared that we had pieced together a few important pieces of our jigsaw there. At the end of our session we fondly embraced each other in the new-found evidence of what we seemed to be to each other.

Fiendish fishermen

Two weeks later, Tom awoke in the early morning of 20th June calling out in a most disconcerting way, so much so that I went to his room to see what was the matter. The time was around six a.m. and I had been awake all night – I don't know why. He had been deeply disturbed by a dream, which he found hard to convey at first but later was able to tell me in enough detail.

"The setting was in a past era," he said, "and I found myself in the entrance of a cave-type dwelling. There were three or four men who were probably fishermen, sitting on what appeared to be a bundle of nets; I assume they were repairing them. The next impressions were particularly vivid. There was a small pool nearby to the men which had a large flat fish flapping about in it; possibly it was a plaice, but judging by its size it was more likely to have been a skate. I noticed it was immersed in only just enough water to keep it alive. I could sense a feeling of something untoward happening here. There was definitely something unsavoury about the company I'd found myself in.

"The fishermen were amazed at my sudden appearance. However, I was especially aware of the man nearest to me. Being of slim build, he was aged about fifty. It seemed that he was their leader. Strangely enough he knew me. I watched him pick up the fish and he then came towards me, jeeringly wafting it in my face. For some obscure reason I felt sickened by this. I became angry, shouting at him to put the wretched thing back.

"Despite the hostile reception I sat down with the leader and recounted the story about the research my partner and I were undertaking. I particularly recall telling him about discovering the whereabouts of the grave and the chilling experience I had. He listened and agreed on each point, seemingly confirming them. I said that I was yet to discover who I was, to which he brusquely replied that he could tell me. But before he could say any more, I suddenly awoke."

As it happened, this disturbing dream encounter oddly affected Tom's mood until nearly noon that day and it was not until then that he was able to convey his ordeal in the detail I have given. At first this was something I could not understand, because I had never known him behave like this before: his whole demeanour had become strangely crabbed and unreasonable. I eventually realised that he might actually have been subjected to more than he wished to relate; had he been in a fight following the incident with the fish and had come off the worse? Just whom had he encountered here? Upon giving my sympathy and support, he began to settle to his old self.

Later the next month, reflecting on this experience, Tom said that he believed the fish in question had actually been a skate. He told me that nowadays there is a law against bringing live female skate inland, since the creature can be used for 'male sexual stimulation'. It now becomes unpleasantly clear what had probably been happening prior to his impromptu appearance and why he felt sickened by having the poor thing wafted in his face. What's more, he thought that he had come upon a den of smugglers and those nets he had seen were probably a front. Unsavoury characters indeed, then.

Over the month of August, I recorded a series of astral trips made by Tom in an intrepid attempt to find the mysterious cave of his dream. By now we had become hooked on delving into this strange encounter. Despite this being liable to misconception – and possible further menaces for that matter – we felt that we should try. Tom was no coward, by any means. So I observed him venture forth into the unknown. What follows is his narrative.

4th August, about 5 a.m.

"Last night I decided to travel back to the cave I found myself in on the 20th of June, so I induced a journey to the era the scene was set in. Once more I found myself in the cave entrance, although this time there was no-one about. I saw a pile of nets which I assume were spares; they lay on the ground as before. Also, I could see the small pool but this time there was no movement in it.

"I tried to move backwards, to leave the entry and venture outside, but for some reason I was unable to. I then awoke."

6th of August

"During the night I made a number of attempts to go back to the cave, but had no success in even reaching it."

8th of August

"Last night I again made repeated attempts, with no success. However, between the hours of 6 and 7 a.m. today I achieved my aim, which was to appear on the beach just outside the cave. From this viewpoint I saw that there were other caves nearby, which I assume were also fishermen's lairs. I could not see very far, as the area was situated in a rocky enclosure, as if I was in a bay. To hazard a guess, it looked like somewhere on the south coast of Cornwall, although I'm not sure." [At this point it occurred to me that Tom's trips were being 'monitored' for his safety, so that he could be in when the others were not about.]

28th of August

"After a few days' break from making these journeys I revisited the cave in the afternoon today. This time I found myself suspended in mid-air, looking down on the location. I think it's East Looe – the shoreline is similar to there whatever."

29th of August

"I made a final journey to the spot, just to be sure. This time I made the trip in the late morning. Once more I found myself on the beach, although it transpired that I was standing further back. This time I was aware of boats moored on the beach and I also had a wider view of the landscape, which revealed the cave I am familiar with situated at the end.

"After my return I saw today's weather report for southern England and I realised that I had seen the place as it is nowadays. It was as if I had taken a day trip in all of ten minutes. I still think it's East Looe."

After looking at an atlas of the south coastal region of Cornwall next day, Tom felt some connection with Truro as well. This did not surprise me as this was a famous port for smugglers and my feeling was that perhaps the Townshends had dealings with the underworld of smuggling in numerous places around the world, maybe even some local to Norfolk. I was later to find that my intuition here was quite right.

I also came to realise that since Tom's initial journeys were made to a past era, in fact he was seeing the landscape as it was then; it has been altered by erosion since then and that cave might no longer exist (see Chapter 7). The one he mentions in his final trip must have been more recent. It was significant because it was based at a port which was renowned for smuggling in olden days, so it was a likely haunt for that horrible fisherman whom he risked meeting again.

Significant women

My thoughts then turned once again to our discoveries at Northampton and to how I could trace the housemaid and the children she had by His Lordship, to whom that astoundingly generous sum had been bequeathed. The most obvious place would be in Charles' Last Will and Testament of course, so to this end I wrote to the Public Records Office to get sight of this document.

On the 11th of July, 1996, I received a copy of the document, which consisted of six pages in all. We became engrossed in deciphering the handwriting, no easy task. After spending much time poring over the pages, looking for mention of the highly favoured housemaid – with no success – we finally identified a passage that seemed to be what we sought. To quote His Lordship:

"Also I give and devise unto Ruth Dimont Widow and her heirs all that Messuage[3] and parcel of land in West Rainham in this County of Norfolk which I have purchased of Harry Goodwyn except the Right and Title belonging to the said Messuage and land and to the Commons and Commonable places in West Rainham aforesaid on the Condition that she or they shall on request of my Son or Grandson in possession of my Honours and family Estate sell and convey to him in fee all the said promises on payment of the said sum of money that I paid to Harry Goodwyn for the said Estate."

We thought that this passage was referring to one of Charles' mistresses, perhaps even the one in question, since this entry is listed amongst the bequests made to his servants. So perhaps we had made another interesting discovery here and found the strumpet whom I had envisaged. It looks as though she received her legacy in property and land; there is no mention of an actual figure here whereas there is in the case of every other beneficiary, which is intriguing.

Later, we would delve into this further by hiring a researcher to look into all the wills made by His Lordship – and there were quite a few. But now I need to describe another very relevant discovery we made, concerning a character who was seemingly unimportant to begin with. I came to find out that she was very significant, as related in a later chapter.

In early 1994, Tom had mentioned in passing how he had briefly seen a vision of what he described as "a very beautiful young lady of about twenty-five years of age, who has some connection with my former life." Besides her apparent beauty, he was aware of her refined and gentle disposition, which suggested to him that she could have been of noble birth. There was little else he knew about her other than that she had died young of an illness of some kind. Unlike the frequent 'visits' made by Audrey, she had appeared to him only once for a few

---

[3] This is a legal term referring to dwellings and the land associated with them.

fleeting moments. She had no message as such, so had therefore been forgotten by us both.

But now it occurred to me that in fact he might have envisaged George Townshend's beloved first wife, Charlotte Compton. I read that she died on the 3rd of September, 1770, at Leixlip Castle in Ireland, towards the end of George's governorship. There's no date for her birth, but from her family tree I estimate that she was in her late thirties when she died. Just what carried her off is a mystery. On the 13th of July, 1996, which as it happened was Tom's birthday, I received a picture of her – portrayed as being very good-looking – and straight away he was taken aback; amazingly, he recognised her without a doubt. It was strange that this awareness of her had only just come to light, though perhaps the time was then right.

Hereafter, I made a few attempts to trace the maiden name of Ruth Dimont, the beneficiary in Charles' will, but it transpired that I was barking up the wrong trees. My intuition was that she had married outside the county of Norfolk, which was in fact right; unfortunately I looked in the wrong places. After rather a barren spell in making any worthwhile discoveries relating to her, things began to move again upon contacting a genealogical researcher who lived locally to Norwich. She agreed to undertake the research about Ruth and her offspring. In all, this spanned a period of three years but I have condensed it into the main discoveries that threw some light on this elusive lady. Much about her early life, however, remained obscure despite this research.

1st of August, 1997

I received news that evidence of the Dimont family was traced in the years of 1753, 1754 and 1758 in the baptism register of West Raynham. Sometime around the early 1750s, Ruth married a Benjamin Dimont and bore him three children in the above years.

The next week I had another report informing me that Ruth had married Thomas Goodwyn, who probably had a connection with the Harry Goodwyn mentioned in the Third Viscount's will. However, there was no mention of her marriage to Benjamin this time.

12th of September, 1997

My researcher was very pleased to forward Ruth Goodwyn's will, also commenting that it is not the usual format of a will. Ruth refers to the remainder of the purchase money for her two cottages and pightle[4] in West Raynham, the amount being £160, which was then due to her from the Right Honourable Viscount Lord Townshend. From this she divided the amount between her husband and two daughters, Mary and Susannah Diamond, spinsters, to share and share alike after her decease.

The testatrix lived and died in Rainham St Margaret (West Raynham) but there was no recorded age of death deposited in the parish of West Raynham. The researcher expressed regret that Benjamin Dimont didn't leave a will, but was interested that he had goods and chattels to the extent that Letters of Administration were required. It was of particular interest that these documents also bore Ruth's signature of acceptance: that a supposed servant of Lord Townshend (though it is uncertain whether she was at the time) could actually write her name, and that as a married woman she made a will, does seem to single her out as someone out of the ordinary.

We had had no luck in finding a record of the marriage of Benjamin and Ruth in other parishes either. My intuition was that she married outside Norfolk, but where remained tantalisingly elusive. Therefore, I chose instead to try to trace Ruth's origins via the baptism registers. These searches proved unfruitful too, probably because she was not from Norfolk, as I came to believe. Perhaps her family had lived in other places before she showed up at Raynham (see Chapter 8). Understandably, I was starting to get just a touch frustrated by now. I only had an inkling that the facts would be found in 'the least likely place' and, as it happened, this turned out to be right; but it took some deciphering and wasn't fully clarified until two and a half years later. Such was the pace the research moved at, I'm afraid.

---

[4] A small field or enclosure.

4

A Surprising Ally

The least likely place

The 14th of April, 1998, was memorable, as I'd just finished moving out of my flat in Madeley, which is based in south Telford. This place lies on the doorstep of the famous Ironbridge Gorge and it is one of the old villages that pre-dates the new town – rather like Arleston in fact. I'd been based here for about eight years in all, although half of this had been spent with Tom, thus making me rather estranged from this community.

After handing over the keys we stopped off at a local pub for a drink, the first time I'd been to the place in about five years. It was intended as a one-off visit initially though it was here that we made a very interesting contact. I'd not had much to do with the place previously, but I'd been acquainted with some of the bar staff and had once heard that the landlady here was interested in mediumship. Over time I'd forgotten about it although I vaguely recall a couple of 'Psychic Nights' being held there.

It was around noon and early in the week when Tom and I paid our visit. We were the only customers present. With hindsight, it appears that we had arrived at an opportune time, for soon after she'd served our order the barmaid – one I used to know – started a conversation about her past life experiences. This was uncanny: she couldn't possibly have known about our quest as we kept it private. She said that she felt at ease divulging this to us since intuition told her that we knew about our previous lives too. It transpired that she was part of a 'development circle' at the local Spiritualist church. This was news to me; whatever her abilities had been before, it appeared they'd been sharpened since I'd last seen her.

She looked at me brightly and declared that she felt a particularly strong connection with me, saying that we had lived around the time of the French Revolution, although she admitted to not being up on historical events much. I felt no such connection with her; however, her remark intrigued me so I asked her to continue. She became absorbed in thought and having paced up and down for a while then told us that illegitimacy was a key factor concerning Tom and myself, and also mutilation.

This, to say the least, was a rather interesting introduction! She went on to say that she was aware my former incarnation had been involved with much mutilation. Then she asked me if I had served in the military, adding that she knew I'd been high-ranking, and whether the colour red had any significance; I told her that it was the colour of the uniform of the English military of the period we were researching and she nodded in agreement. Further, she knew that Tom and I had had a number of former lives together and that in one of them I had killed him. At some point following this, I recall that she gave me a knowing look and asked me if I – meaning George – had been "sexually active," meaning promiscuous. I had to admit he had been; this meant a lot to her and it caused some amusement between us.

Having paced around a little more, she was able to tell us that in our former lives Tom and I had been connected from childhood and had grown up together. She said there was a strong feeling of love, from the heart, and also that jealousy and ill-feeling had surrounded us from those early years. All this was uncannily in agreement with what we had found out, but there was absolutely no way she could have known about any of this from us, or elsewhere in this world anyway.

Then she continued by relating her own former life experiences. She told us that for about ten years she had had a recurring dream in which she is conscious of being a young girl of about twelve years of age, standing alone in a doorway. She has travelled many miles to get to this place, maybe fifty or more. The doorway is in a street and it is growing dark. She can see the light from what look like gas or perhaps oil street lamps; rain stings the air and she draws a shawl closer around her to guard against the chill. She is holding a piece of paper bearing some writing, perhaps telling of her identity or perhaps the address she's seeking. She knows she must find a specific place in this locality, for there is a man of influence here who can help her.

This vision has made an enduring impression in her memory and she has always wondered about its meaning and longed to discover who she was, but after meeting us today she knew it had some connection with us. Upon hearing this we asked her name and she replied that it was Liz, known as 'Young Liz' at the pub because she was the landlady's daughter. She's of the same age as myself, being just a few months older. We arranged to see her again.

Further to this meeting we arranged to see her at her flat in the early evening two weeks later. I took my diary so that she could read just how accurate she had been during our discourse in the pub. When we met she was eager to take things further; normally she did not feel so at ease talking to strangers, but she felt a strong empathy with us. She sat in her chair and I passed the diary to her; oddly, as I handed over the manuscript, I felt a chill in the surrounding atmosphere. She surveyed the passages I had written and became increasingly enthused. The time we spent together could be compared to a gushing fountain, with thoughts and insights just pouring from both of us. It was incredible, this former stranger bringing three years of research to life with such down-to-earth clarity. Anyone would have become engrossed in it.

For some reason I picked up on comments she made about the instigator of the scandal. The term that describes her as an "uneducated country wench" had some familiarity for Liz and she looked up at me with a beaming smile as she quoted the phrase. It was almost as if this was a smile of acknowledgement. I noticed that she mistook the word 'country' for 'county' and I draw attention to this as it seemed as if this word in particular had a meaning for her. Also, she read out loud that the woman had died slowly and painfully of an illness, and straight away Liz declared that it was syphilis and gonorrhoea, with all the assurance of someone who had known her personally.

She observed the portrait of George that I showed her and cheekily commented that I haven't changed much over the centuries! Following this, her face glowed somewhat and she expressed she had borne much love for George during that incarnation. Towards the later part of the evening, she referred to another incarnation that she knew Tom and had lived through and claimed to see alternating images of me as George and also as the woman I'd been in the life before that, commenting that Tom and I had always been together through these lives. We believed that she was right about all of this, as we also felt we knew about the life before George and his friend. All in all it was a compelling meeting and we felt that our new found association would be ongoing. Previously, there had been no-one else with whom we had this degree of empathy concerning our quest.

Another two weeks later, on the 13th of May, 1998, we visited Liz again during the morning an hour or so before she went to work. She was in the same convivial spirits as before, although on this occasion her familiarity switched to Tom and she gave us a few more insights on the lives we had led as half-brothers. Tom was able to link with much of what she said, for example he could also recall stealing a fruit bun from the kitchen. We were already aware that he was a likeable rogue in his former childhood. She told us that Tom and I got on famously together: George used to love going fishing with his brother and doing the things boys generally do together. However, as we had grown older we had become more competitive and a rift started to develop, especially when it came to the opposite sex. She regarded Tom saucily and remarked that she could see him in many a hay loft. What is more, Tom said that he had recollections of this too. I felt reassured by his agreement, as I couldn't relate to any of it. Jack-the-lad indeed. Sadly, though, I was to find later that he was no competition otherwise and it's my belief that therein lay the rift.

The ghost woman and the Madam

After telling us these things, Liz remarked that somehow she felt she had been kept away from us, since she was looking on these scenes as if she were a ghost in the background. This seemed intriguing when I first heard it and I came to realise that this was indeed probably because she had been (see Chapter 8).

Subsequently Liz asked us if we had any idea who she had been. We had to admit that we didn't, whereupon she told us that she now knew more about her experience as the young girl in the doorway. She was aware of being gaunt and heavily pregnant; in fact, she was so near her time that she went into labour on the street. It was the girl's first pregnancy. Liz described how "a haggard crone of an old woman" came to her aid, but then took the baby away from her, insisting that it was the best thing to do. That was the last she saw of her firstborn. Liz went on to tell us that the girl felt much anger towards a young English soldier by whom she had become pregnant. He had always assured her that he would care for her, but had abandoned her in her time of need. At this point Liz told us that the girl was Irish, the scene was somewhere in Ireland and Dublin came to her mind, since she was aware of it being near to the coast. Could this be the 'county' wench? I then asked if she knew the soldier's age and she said he had been roughly around the late teens or early twenties.

The conversation turned and she began she began talking about George's personality once more, commenting that he had liked to show a tough exterior when really he was soft. With this, I showed her some more portraits of George and his family that I had brought for her to see. She steadily perused each one, commenting on the characters of each one.

However, when she came to the one that Tom had identified as the murderer, she stopped. As I mentioned before, George's expression is cold and ruthless in this portrait. However, Liz gave a knowing smile and fondly caressed the picture as she held it on her lap; over and over again, she shook her head and stroked the picture, cooing that really he was as soft as a kitten. From this we got the distinct impression that, whatever her relationship had been with George, it must have been of a rather intimate nature.

The time came for Liz to get ready for work and she disappeared into the bathroom to begin dressing her hair. After a while she emerged with her hair pinned up into a bouffant style, quite different to how we had seen her before. There was also a strange air about her, as if she were on the brink of going into a trance. She said that 'something told her' that with her hair like this we would recognise her from before. At this point I thought she was Ruth, Tom's former mother. Maybe it was because I was eager to find a solution to the puzzle but whatever the case it seemed to fit and the three of us were satisfied with the suggestion. Liz especially could easily accept that she had been a peasant who had become a lord's mistress and, in her own words, "slept her way to the top". With this, we dropped her off at the pub and she went on her way with a distinct air of satisfaction and pride.

Another two weeks later, we called on Liz during her free time and offered to take her out for the day. We suggested visiting Arleston Manor as we were keen to see her reactions there. Before leaving, we spent about an hour with her at her flat, once again listening to her latest revelations. She had experienced many more insights since our last meeting and was keen to tell them all.

She was able to give more information about her life in Ireland. She agreed that she had been born into a peasant family and as a young girl had gained employment as a domestic servant in a large house; a man called Byron or Bryan was significant here. She told us of a man she had encountered in spirit during her sleep who showed her a map she recognised to be of Ireland. He had made repeated efforts to point out her place of origin, but despite this she had awoken with only a vague awareness that it was situated in a small corner of a county next to another place, which she could only define as beginning with the prefix 'Kil'.

Her job had entailed spending a total of eighteen hours a day at the house, serving meals and performing general domestic duties, all pretty routine stuff except that it sounds as if she virtually lived there. Following this, she looked at me awkwardly and remarked that from what she was about to say we would probably get the impression that her former persona had been "a slut". She admitted that she used to flaunt herself at all the men in the household, servants and masters alike, so she could gain favours. She seems to have been very popular with everyone.

After making this admission, she continued with more details about her time as Lord Townshend's mistress, informing us that he provided her with a house in which she 'serviced his needs'. He liked her for her earthy sense of humour, which was a refreshing escape from the stuffiness of the high society of the day. We assumed this was just one of her many attractions, whereupon she added with a glint in her eye that they had also been good lovers, remarking heartily on Townshend's prowess in this area.

Later, Liz went on to describe a vivid vision of a woman, which had happened one morning since our last visit. The impressions had been distinct and left her thinking that the encounter was of some importance. She thought the woman to be of forty years of age and, judging by her clothes, she appeared well-off, say, eighteenth century middle class. She was quite plump with long dark hair flowing down her back. However, she had a disturbingly raucous demeanour, not surprising really as it transpired she was the Madam of a brothel.

Liz witnessed a scene at the establishment she ran. Her first impression was that the place was squalid. She claimed to see a handful of young girls, clad in what appeared to be bodices and stockings, which were equally as filthy as the place they worked in. Next she related a very unpleasant incident in which the Madam bullied a young girl of about fifteen into attending to a client. The girl was a virgin while the man was old and lecherous with an abundance of warts on his face. She stood there petrified, dreading the prospect of having to serve him. In response, the Madam let out a rasping laugh and pushed her towards the man, forcing her to her fate.

This horrible laugh clearly grated on Liz, as she visibly shuddered upon mentioning it. Her vision showed the Madam in a number of lewd acts at the brothel, all of which were too lurid to go into any detail about. Liz pondered this for a while, musing that maybe the practice was somewhere in London. At any rate, after this experience it was her belief that at some time she must have been a whore.

On this high note we set off on our tour. Of the three places we visited, the one that left the greatest impression on her was Arleston Manor. Like Tom, she also felt a familiarity with the place and was angry that it now stands as a condemned building. She recalled being in this part of Shropshire with her children in that era. The outing was something of an anti-climax in a sense but we enjoyed it nevertheless. What we learned at her flat had produced the best results.

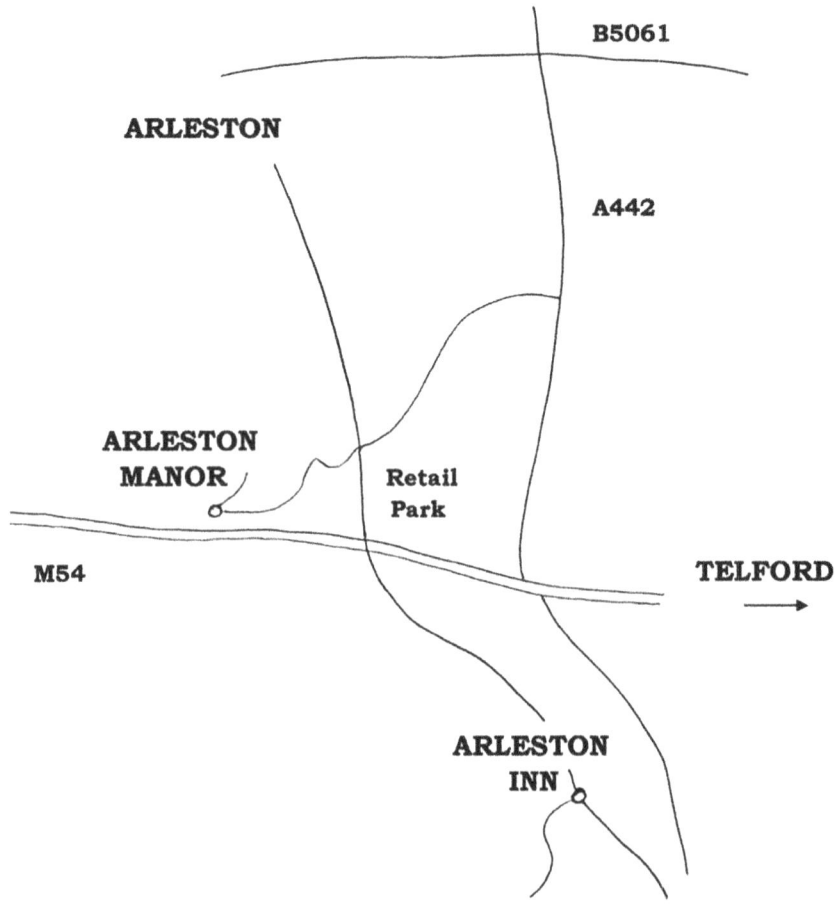

ARLESTON, SHROPSHIRE

The Irish Townsends

I did some more research at the library on the 8th of June. Upon looking through the Dictionary of National Biography, I noticed an entry relating to a family called Townsend (note the spelling) at a place called Castletownshend in Ireland. This was news to me. By looking at a map it is possible to see that this is a small village situated on the south-west coast of County Cork. In fact, you could say that it is in "the corner of a county," as Liz had described, and indeed it lies adjacent to another county called Killarney. What a discovery! The entry started with Richard Townsend, 1618–1692, a parliamentary colonel who, according to tradition, was descended from the Townshends of Rainham, Norfolk. He was married twice, leaving seven sons and four daughters. The eldest surviving son, Bryan, served with the English army at the battle of the Boyne, and was an ancestor of the family of Townsend at Castletownshend. This seemed an extraordinary confirmation of Liz's dream.

Some time later that month, I did some more research about Bryan and found that there was no date for his birth. However, the battle of the Boyne was in 1695 and he died in 1727, leaving his estates to his son Richard, 168?–1742. It is possible that this fits with the approximate date of the alleged account Liz gave. When I told her about these findings and mentioned Bryan serving at the battle of the Boyne, we exchanged a halting stare: this certainly pressed a button with us. Strangely, as I spoke, we both felt a distinct chill flowing in the atmosphere between us, almost like an invisible river in our midst. It was clear that my recent researches fitted her insights. On that note, Tom and I made arrangements to pay another visit to Tamworth Castle, this time accompanied by Liz, since we felt sure she could make a valuable contribution there.

Tamworth Castle revisited

We set off on the trip to Tamworth with great anticipation of making further progress. Our first port of call, however, was to Tom's business associates who were based in Tettenhall, Wolverhampton. Over the time we had known them they had expressed some interest in our claims about reincarnation and we were keen for them to meet our new companion. She made a good enough impression here with her psychic abilities, especially with the secretary.

Liz and I sat alone together in Reception chatting about her latest insights. The conversation turned and while discussing the scene of the supposed assault at Tamworth Castle, quite unexpectedly she exclaimed that it did not take place in the kitchen and in fact it didn't happen within the castle at all for that matter. Well, this disputed the whole purpose of the trip and I wished she'd told us sooner. However, we decided not to mention it to Tom and to carry on regardless.

From Wolverhampton we continued on our way to Tamworth via Cannock and Lichfield. Upon reaching the crossroads at Pipehill near Lichfield, we unexpectedly made a detour through a place called Wall, which is a rural district with a network of narrow winding lanes. For some inexplicable reason, Tom drove the car straight ahead on a road he hadn't taken before. En route, Liz experienced a panic attack, which she suppressed long enough for us not realise what was happening at first. But it became so bad that we had to stop for a while for her to recover herself.

Later, while chain-smoking cigarettes, she told us that she had re-lived an incident connected to this place. She had been in the company of George and his half-brother; the moment was an extremely unpleasant one for her, as she vividly remembered trying to escape from 'us'. We caught up with her, violently restraining her with such force that she was almost choked. This was an extreme way for Tom's former incarnation to treat his mother! "You both betrayed me," she said miserably. She didn't know what it was all about. Realising that this experience was traumatic for Liz, we stayed put for a while to give her a chance to settle down.

When she felt better, I asked whether by any chance she knew her age at the time of this incident. She was able to tell me that she was around her early twenties and that we were all around a similar age. That being so, it doesn't tally that she was Ruth, although we kept an open mind. Upon approaching Tamworth, the image of the castle loomed before us, an unforgettably prominent feature on the land-scape. The site held much significance for all three of us. Regretfully, it relates to what we believe to be a bygone tragedy, nevertheless the desire to explore the past was strong and we ventured forth undeterred.

Upon our arrival we began the ascent up the long pathway leading towards the shell keep. It was peak season and the place was thronged with people, quite different to our earlier visit. When we reached the top, I realised that I needed to return to the car to get my purse and when I returned I found them waiting beside the thirteenth century gatehouse – it's the back gate, basically. Originally built as a look-out position, this site is a ruin that had recently been excavated. To be honest, neither Tom nor I had noticed it before, which is not surprising as there's not much of it left. It was not open to the public, but it was possible to look down onto what resembled a mini-courtyard that was guarded by two watchtowers at the front.

This time it was Tom who was appearing disturbed; leaning on the safety barrier, he gazed down in silence at the gatehouse courtyard as if he'd been pole-axed. In my absence, they had learned that the assault had actually taken place here and Tom was now feeling the vibrations of the trauma. So Liz's earlier insight was clarified here, thankfully. I believe it was meant to be that I should return to the car for a while.

After this episode Liz and I toured around the castle while Tom took a rest. It really had taken a lot out of him. As it happened, Liz said that she also felt bad vibrations as we descended the stairs in the tower, although nothing like what happened at Wall. By coincidence, this was the same place where I had felt particularly nauseous before, though not this time. In fact, I had no bad experiences throughout the whole trip – not that I'm disappointed.

Years later, a friend of mine who is a medium picked up on what he described as being 'a forgotten passageway' that leads from the back gatehouse to the kitchen. I had made a point of not disclosing anything I knew about the murder scene to this friend. Does this support Tom's insight of the whereabouts of the murder scene? And what to make of the wooden table that he said was used for the meat deliveries? It all seems to fit together well, so it appears that there is a significance with the kitchen after all. Sometimes, though, it seems to take a few people to sort it out fully.

As we anticipated, the day had proved very successful and we rounded it off by inviting her round to our place for a coffee. Soon after our return from taking her home, another spooky encounter happened that we found a bit unnerving. As Tom sat relaxing in his easy chair, he glimpsed the figure of a hooded monk outside through the window in the front door. What did he want? No, not today thank you… The encounter was a brief one though; moving from right to left, the figure crossed the pathway just before the porch, whereupon it disappeared through the garage wall adjacent to it.

As if this had been prophetic, a few days after this a relative to whom Liz had been especially close passed away and we didn't see her for a while. I recall her telling us over the phone that she needed space in order to mourn the loss. We gave her our condolences of course. During that time, I awoke one morning with a strong taste of cigarettes in my mouth, which unfortunately remained with me throughout the day – neither of us smoke. From time to time I also caught a whiff of what smelled like a full ashtray in the hall, near the front door; it was like her calling card. When I saw her again I was to learn that recently she had been smoking even more heavily than usual, as solace in her bereavement. She was pleased to know that I had been able to make some kind of link with her, as she also had much with me. This was interesting, as formerly I'd only ever had such empathy with Tom.

Sinister visions

Sometime during this month, Liz gave us snippets of a couple of experiences which she believed showed that she had been Tom's mother. In one she was aware of giving birth to him. The child was named Benjamin Franklin. He received prestige from his father simply because his mother was a favoured lover at the time; as Tom had once said, he had been a love-child. Later research proved that, indeed, His Lordship was always generous with his illegitimate offspring for that matter: note the wills of the Third Viscount Townshend, although there is no mention of a Benjamin Franklin in any. Could he also have been out of favour when his father began making them?

Liz also recalled a time when she was on board a ship crossing over to England. The voyage was a rough one and she remembered holding onto a broken beam, flooded all around by seawater. She was aware of her child hanging on nearby too. I was to discover that elements of these insights were true, although there were a few crossed wires, as I'll explain in the next chapter. This was not unusual. However, I could trace no mention of any such member of the Townshend family for that time. Was the record deliberately removed by any chance? Certain records are definitely missing. Perhaps there is some reference amongst those papers that were sold to scholars and suchlike earlier last century. I have an intuition that something will come to light one day, somehow, some way…

The most disturbing of all the visions that Liz had around this time was when she encountered the Madam once again. We called on her one morning to find her in a rather rough state, which we found disquieting. She told us it was because she had had a very disturbing encounter with a spirit earlier on, rather similar to Tom's experience with the fisherman. She had been visited by the Madam; it was a hideous encounter as the creature came towards her coughing and hacking violently. She gargled up blood and spat it out, cackling that Liz was none the wiser as to who she was formerly. "You're nowhere near it, dearie." This stuck chillingly in her memory upon waking.

This was very difficult for Liz to relate; however she gave enough detail for us to realise that the Madam had considerable meaning for her. When we told her about Tom's ordeal of the year before, it transpired that she too had a link with smugglers. She said she had once seen the Madam walking along a beach to meet up with her husband, who had made acquisitions from smuggling that day. It wouldn't be at all surprising if the Madam and the fisherman were linked actually – they were equally horrible characters.

Keeping in touch with Liz became increasingly difficult for a while, due to personal problems, but sometime around late July we were able to make contact with her again and paid her another visit. This time she had yet more disturbing news to relate, but she had reservations about disclosing it in Tom's presence; she was too ashamed, as she thought him to be her former son. So she confided to me, rather awkwardly, that… she had been the brothel-keeper. Regretfully, it was her own former self with whom she'd experienced the nightmarish encounters. It was a harrowing revelation for her and she had difficulties coming to terms with it. After hearing this I had to sympathise; it would have upset anyone. Yet it came as no surprise to Tom when I later passed on the news; he just nodded and replied flatly that he had suspected it for some time.

Apart from this, Liz was entering a rather turbulent phase in this life and later that evening it became clear that it was best if we withdrew. So we drove away with the distinct feeling that our meetings with her would become more rare – and indeed so it transpired.

5

Wonderland

This chapter marks the beginning of a whole new tree of knowledge, which opened up over the next six months. It could even be likened to a Pandora's Box. Whichever way you choose to look at it, my life was about to change radically. Never again would I look at life in the same way – nor indeed could I! Yes, paranormal experiences do tend to leave a question mark for many, but I assure you that I tell it exactly as it happened and, as ever, others must form their own opinions.

Firstly, I should include an account of our professional researcher's work and describe what came to light between the months of July and November of 1998. Her contribution is worthwhile, as it validates the comments I made earlier about the housemaid's offspring in Sherson's book. There's evidence of Ruth under a different surname, which is interesting, and we also got evidence of another very significant name from this research, which must not be overlooked.

Initially, our researcher enthusiastically reported that she had come upon a folder full of wills made by Charles Townshend (1700–1764) between 1754–1763. She particularly noticed that there were three men who kept turning up. There is Peter Stringer along with his daughters, and his final housekeeper Elizabeth Stringer; but in later wills he makes it very clear that he wants children by Elizabeth Walker, his former housekeeper, to benefit. Failing that, we have the mysterious Charles and Henry Browne of Norwich.

Ruth was introduced later, possibly after the death of her husband Benjamin in 1758. The wording was then changed in her favour, in a codicil to the main will. From various papers it would appear that both Ruth and Benjamin were quite highly valued by Charles and appeared consistently through the years of 1754–1763, and then again in the final will, that went to probate. But at some time between March and the final will, dated the 16th of October 1763, Elizabeth Walker 'Housekeeper' and her brother Edmund were completely cut out and Elizabeth Stringer took her place. It was noted that others also feature in the wills at various times, especially the three daughters of Peter Stringer, who seemed to be special.

Our researcher agreed that Ruth's legacy appeared to have been very generous, as only Charles' legitimate children were left any property. Upon looking in turn at Ruth's will of 1776, the question arises whether Charles' eldest son, George, bought the property back from her. After reading this report, Tom declared that the name Stringer certainly rang a bell.

In the November of this year we were told that a Ruth Hartwell had been found to be listed among Charles Townshend's accounts 1738–1763. The questions is, was this the Ruth who had been his former mistress? I would say so, in view of what came to light the following year. In any case, the research now succeeded in proving that Elizabeth Walker was indeed another of Charles' mistresses: together with the generous entries alongside her name in the accounts and also in the draft wills, it is clear that this woman did very well as a 'housekeeper'.

We found it intriguing that in Charles' eighth and tenth wills, of 1759 and 1760, he bequeathed three hundred pounds each to the mysterious infants Charles and Henry Browne of the City of Norwich. This sum was intended for Elizabeth Walker to bring them up, "unless she has a child before or within nine months" of his death. What was he thinking here? Reading further, it can be seen that in 1763 he bequeathed an amazing five thousand pounds (not fifty thousand) to Elizabeth Walker and to one Edward Browne. It looked very much like we'd traced the three children to whom Sherson referred. But by October 1763, Lord Townshend had completely cut her out of his will – though not their children – and had also terminated her employment. What had she done?

There was little else worth mentioning regarding this research until the April of the following year, although the findings made then were worthwhile. But for future reference, it's worth noting the Stringer family as they will come into play again further on.

Charles Townshend, 3rd Viscount of Raynham
Courtesy of The Peerage

A summary of the main characters referred to here

Peter Stringer — He was a loyal servant of Charles, Third Viscount Townshend.

Elizabeth Stringer — Peter's daughter and Charles' final housekeeper.

Elizabeth Walker — Charles' earlier housekeeper and also his mistress. It seems that she had three sons by him, the mysterious infants *Charles* and *Henry Browne* of Norwich and later one *Edward Browne* to whom Charles bequeathed five thousand pounds for Elizabeth to bring up.

Benjamin Dimont — Another valued servant of Charles who often appears in His Lordship's draft wills.

Ruth Dimont (nee Barnes) — Benjamin's widow, bequeathed property in Charles' final will. Ruth might have been a former mistress to Charles, by whom she allegedly begat *Benjamin Franklin*, although there are no surviving records of this.

Ruth Hartwell — She appears in early household accounts as a housemaid and might also may have a significant connection to the puzzle.

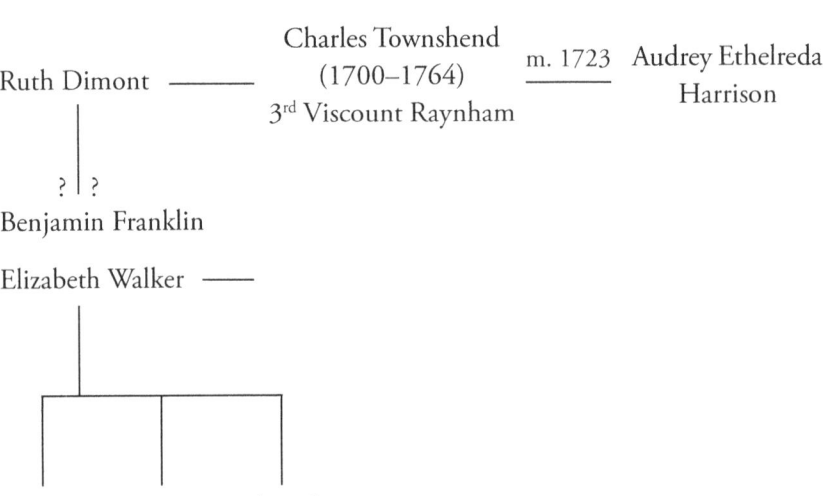

The truth about Liz

Now we come to the events of late September, 1998, which mark the beginning of the profound 'tree of knowledge' mentioned earlier. It was late in the afternoon of the 22nd of September, a day I shall always remember. As I lay alone on my bed, somehow I could sense the 'vibrations' of a spirit woman who wished to make contact with me. This was my first experience of being able to communicate with the spirit world. Initially I thought it was Audrey, as I felt she was from that era, but I was surprised to find her reply was negative. I paused for a moment and then asked if she were Charlotte, George's first wife, and her reply was "Yes." I felt a sudden rush of guilt, as I knew that George had treated her badly. However, she indicated that there were no ill-feelings, as all that was long in the past.

A couple of days later I itched to find out more. Firstly, had our friend Liz really been Ruth Dimont? To my surprise, the answer was "No, indeed she wasn't." I felt rather dismayed about this. So I asked whether she had any connection with us at all, whereupon I was relieved to find that she did. Charlotte confirmed that Liz had worked at a Townshend residence as a 'domestic servant', although it became clear that she had been a prostitute in fact. She was an Irish peasant girl and she had indeed been a mistress, although it was not to Charles. So if Liz had not been Ruth, did this mean that we were yet to meet her? My confidante was very definite that we would and, what's more, it wouldn't be long before we did. (It turned out that she had returned in this life as Tom's eldest daughter! Well, the two characters were very much alike so no wonder there was confusion here. To my amusement my confidante couldn't agree more.)

The following day, I recalled Liz telling us that the father of her first child had been a young English soldier and that she had been twelve years of age at the time. I felt the need to ask about this and both points were confirmed. It was also true that he had abandoned her in her time of need. After a while it suddenly dawned on me that it had been George who was responsible. This was the turning point – he most certainly was. Eureka! I was very pleased to have sorted out which Townshend was being referred to. My confidante was in full agreement when I commented that it was like-father-like-son. This was uncanny, as even the soldier's age fitted with the account; he would have been approaching twenty at the beginning of his military career.

It was also confirmed that Liz's former incarnation had lived in England and that she had been around the age of twenty when this happened. It transpired that she had been a mistress to both George and to Benjamin Dimont, and had later been 'betrayed' by both. The incident at Wall did have a bearing on this. I was now kicking myself for not realising that this point alone meant she could not have been Benjamin's mother, as the ages just didn't fit.

After conferring with Charlotte for a while longer, I gained more insight about the former character whom we now knew as Liz. She had indeed been a 'Lolita', who from an early age had used sex to get what she wanted, much to the disdain of the rest of her family; apparently, she was what is best described as a 'black sheep'. Contrary to what Liz had told us – that she had loved George in her previous life – Charlotte insisted that this was never the case. The feelings that Liz recalled were merely an infatuation at best.

Reflecting now on Tom's initial story of April 1994, which was the starting point for all this research, I thought about the points I had picked up on during our first meeting with Liz at her flat; I wondered, had Liz been the young woman who instigated the fateful scandal? The reply was a definite "Yes." Now things were really coming together; I could clearly see her motives and everything fitted perfectly.

I gathered that soon after the murder the young woman began blackmailing George, although it appears that she did this only once. Once was enough, as she succeeded in getting thousands of pounds, something like £12,000, which was a vast amount of money in those days. Later, she did indeed become the Madam of a brothel and she was involved with smugglers around this time too. Liz had suggested that she had died of venereal disease, but it transpired that in fact it had been from consumption. This explains the grisly encounter in which Liz had envisaged the Madam coughing up blood. But she did also have venereal disease and was in a terrible state when she died.

Realising that I had spent quite a long time absorbed in the life of Madam Sin, I thought it best to wind up the discourse now, especially as I also realised that much if not all of this could not be proved with any tangible evidence. Even so, I just had to ask a few more questions about this woman's married life, if she ever had been married, that is. I found that around her mid-twenties she had been involved with a publican, or something like that, who had engaged in illicit practices to boost his income. Seems like they were 'birds of a feather' in that respect. Following this, I suddenly had the idea that the young woman had been a relative of Peter Stringer, which turned out to be right. (This must have come from Charlotte, as I wasn't focused on him at all.) But she's not among those who were included in Charles' will though, more's the pity. Charlotte must have been grateful when I ended this session, but much had been learned.

A couple of days later I had the persistent feeling that there was yet more that I should know about our heroine. This was becoming an obsession. Firstly, what part of Ireland had she come from? Liz had thought that it was Dublin but this was not so, nor was it anywhere nearby. The place in question was in fact Castletownshend and she had worked briefly at the manor house there, where she first met George. I wondered about the young girl in the doorway whom Liz had talked of and where this had been. It took a while but eventually I was able to deduce that it was twenty miles due east from Castletownshend along the coast. By looking at a map I was able to identify the place as being Clonakilty, without doubt. I'd never heard of it. Tom and I promised ourselves that we would visit this part of southern Ireland one day, as we felt sure we would find something there.

At this point, Tom's sighting of the hooded figure crossing the pathway to our front door came back to me and my mind went into overdrive. Was 'the man of influence' to whom Liz had referred a priest or something like that, and was the place she had sought been a respite or a hospital by any chance? Indeed it was so, in both cases. It made me wonder if there are still records of there being such a place, and Charlotte told me that there are.

Upon young Mistress Stringer's arrival in the alley, the scene was as Liz had described it. How terrible was that? The old woman who took the baby was a local peasant who was passing by. This place was renowned as a place of respite for unmarried mothers so it was probably commonplace to find young women in the same plight as she had been on that cold and wet evening. I became curious to know more about Mistress Stringer's 'helper' and I learned that she was not connected to the hospital at all; no, she was in fact a procurer of infants and young children for the use of wealthy paedophiles – this was horrific! I felt stunned and Charlotte also had difficulty telling me about it. Moreover, this was not the only child that George had fathered and neglected. I felt sick…

The wretched condition that Mistress Stringer had been in at that time was for no other reason other than that her family had been too poor to feed her. However, she did receive food and shelter at the hospital until she was able to make her way home. Her early life had been a harsh one indeed. Who would have been an Irish peasant in that era? By now it was getting rather late and I felt that I should take a break from this and I got the feeling that Charlotte was very grateful for this too, as things had taken an unpleasant turn. She is of such a gentle disposition, just as Tom had said.

But later that day Charlotte was happy to confide to me some more about Mistress Stringer, as I still had a few more questions. Soon after splitting up with George, she came across to England to live in the Midlands. Walsall came to mind, but the feeling was unclear and I could tell that this was not exactly the right place. Tom and I looked at a map of the area around Walsall hoping for a clue, and something told me that Cannock was significant. Perhaps she'd lived there?

A couple of weeks later we visited the Records and Research Library at Stafford, as this is where all old documents about Cannock are kept. We scanned through the parish registers for entries under the name Stringer based in and around Cannock for that era, and I found one: Thomas, son of Samuel Stringer of Great Wyrley (near Walsall), buried on the 15th of June, 1760. Was this just a strange coincidence?

I couldn't trace whether he was from Ireland, though, because there are no such documents: Ireland came under the English Crown in those days. Even so, we felt we had achieved something that day and it had been worthwhile quizzing Charlotte about it. It now became clear why she had guided me to Cannock.

At a later time, I traced more members of this family in this area and it certainly is thought-provoking. There's no birth or baptism record of Thomas' father, Samuel, in this whole county and none for Thomas either. A county-wide search for his parents' marriage drew a blank too. What's more, there are no more listings of burials for any of them, yet there were three other children (see Chapter 8). So where did they come from and where did they go? That seemed to be as far as we could go with this research.

Recycled royals

Much to my amusement, later this month I was to find that some of Tom's business associates in this world also had connections with us in our past lives. To begin with, this seemed a bit of a joke even to me, although Charlotte assured me it was true. Well, admittedly we had been very loyal to the Managing Director and his family for a few years, through thick and thin in fact. I was now prompted to recall former spirit messages we had received, urging us to stay loyal to them through the difficult times regardless of what happened. So on the strength of this, I proceeded to find out more.

It came to me that the Managing Director had formerly been the illustrious parliamentary minister, Earl Granville. Well, yes I could see it might be so and Tom especially could easily accept it – the significance of Leveson Gower was immediately clarified for him. He had known the boss before he began working for him at a financial company and they had always been great comrades. By a twist of fate, they had met up again in recent years and taken part in a couple of business ventures together. It transpired that other members of his family were also reincarnations of distinguished people of the eighteenth century. Surprisingly, they were very interested to hear this.

The man's wife had formerly been Henry Pelham, who strongly opposed Earl Granville in parliament, so it's really quirky that they were married in this life. Next there was his son, Andrew, who was formerly the Duke of Cumberland; then there was his secretary and close friend, who was formerly Princess Amelia and the Duke's eldest sister. Tom agreed that there was a noticeable empathy between these two and furthermore they knew it themselves; they did have quite a few things in common actually.

To think, we had reincarnated royalty in our midst. Did this mean we had to bow whenever we entered the office now? The secretary commented that she had once dreamed that this had been so. We also learned that Andrew had a keen interest in the military when he was at school and it was something he wanted to pursue upon finishing his education; however, he lost interest when he found that he couldn't start at the level he wanted to. Was this the Duke in him coming out? Furthermore, I read that Earl Granville (the boss) had had a political liaison with Princess Amelia (his secretary) at some stage; perhaps it could be said that this still applied.

Yes, all this may seem a bit far-fetched to some, but for Tom and me it brought a very heartening conclusion to the events happening at the business around that time. Whatever support we gave, we did so gladly as we knew it was meant to be.

Introducing James

Around the last week of that month I realised that Charlotte had taken a back seat when a rather more robust character came to the fore. It was late at night, Tom had gone to bed and I was sitting alone in the lounge. Suddenly I could sense the presence of a spirit man. To start with there was a forthright, almost military quality to his 'vibrations', which firmly established that I was in touch with someone quite different. I felt a bit wary but soon found that he intended no harm. After a while I realised that he was someone who had been connected with George's military career.

Had he been in the battle of Culloden? "No." However, he had been in the battle of Quebec. Was he General Wolfe? "No", but he "should have had his job!" Was he one of the brigadiers who rivalled George for the leadership after Wolfe died? This was so and it then became clear what he had meant. Shortly afterwards, I picked up that he was Scottish and it turned out to be right.

Over the next fortnight I tried to find out who my latest confidant was. Reading up about battles in that era, I was drawn to a George Murray who had fought in the battle of Culloden. There was just something about the name and my new friend told me this was "partly right." This was a puzzle – what did he mean by that? Later it dawned on me that he was actually referring to his name. After studying the Dictionary of National Biography it finally clicked that he was in fact James Murray (1721–1794) who, as he had said, fought in the battle of Quebec. (I recall that his response was very hale and hearty: "Well done, you've finally cracked it. Not before time either.") Later, moreover, I was amused to discover that he had adopted 'Partly' as his nickname. Reading further, I noted he had for a time been the governor of Minorca, and was then nicknamed 'Old Minorca'. He could identify with this and by his response I could tell that he looked back on the period with pride. I have to say that I felt rather honoured to be connected with such prominent people of that century.

Soon after making these discoveries, I became aware of his presence on a few occasions. Sometimes during the day, when I was busy doing something, I would feel a slight chill in the atmosphere close by, just to let me know that he was looking in for a while. There were also other occasions, during the early hours of the morning as I slept, that I encountered him in the spirit world.

James Murray
© The National Portrait Gallery, London

On our first meeting, I saw that he was short in height and rather stocky. It came across that he preferred to introduce himself as a down-to-earth person, as he appeared wearing casual twentieth century clothes, a pair of jeans and a tee-shirt – nothing like the image of the elevated position he had held during his time on Earth. His personality, however, was unmistakable. I was to find that he had a warm and friendly disposition and there was a distinct feel of protectiveness about him as he guided me through what I can best describe as a dream in which he reviewed the recent events of my life. He referred to the areas where I had made my worst mistakes. Even upon waking, I found that I had to agree about this. He showed me the current structure of my life, part of which had been' engineered' – my meeting with Tom. He also made suggestions about changing my job and I was relieved to hear it was nothing too radical.

James met up with me a few times during the months of November and December. Usually this was in the early hours of the morning. Sometimes his messages came through to me by images and situations, similar to a virtual reality setting. In others, I clearly saw him in person and we spoke to each other as if we were on Earth. Each time, he presented himself as either a modern day squaddie or as a skinhead! He always played down his image.

I would awake from these extraordinary encounters with a feeling of awe. I was having similar experiences as those that Liz and Tom had related – although mine were rather more cordial. Giving it more thought, I realised that this really was nothing new as I had had similar encounters during my adolescence, although those weren't friendly. I was now getting a fuller picture of what happens upon entering 'the twilight zone'.

Postscript

One afternoon sometime in November, Tom and I met up with Liz again for the first time in about four months. It turned out we were also in the company of her boyfriend, and the circumstances were quite different from our former meetings. On this occasion, unfortunately, we were visiting her in a sanatorium – she was drying out from alcohol addiction again. It came as no surprise to find that it was not the first time she had been a patient there either. Yet she appeared relatively well and we spent an hour or so with her at the coffee bar in the hospital grounds.

I told her of our recent discoveries about who she had been in her former life and she looked at me astonished. So did her boyfriend, and I could tell that he thought we had come to the right place. When Liz heard that she had been George's mistress, the feeling of intimacy she had felt became amusingly clear after a while and we had a good laugh about it. It was just as well her boyfriend took it in good part too. At length we departed, hoping for an improvement in her health.

6

My Journey into Light

Around this time I underwent the first of numerous encounters, spanning a period of four years, the effects of which were to change radically both our lives for all time. Indeed, these were the most harrowing experiences of our lives and, in a spiritual sense, the most triumphant. I can truly say that as I now relate the following episodes I am a reformed person. The wrongdoings of the past life – and also of the present one – became agonisingly clear and I came to realise that we are all 'sinners in the sight of God'; none of us is perfect and, whatever our faith, I came to learn that we are all spiritual beings at varying levels of progression. Sometimes, regardless of however hard it may be, we have to make this progression and my message is intended to give hope to those who suffer – as we did.

Touched by evil

It was mid-December and in the early hours of one morning I had a strange dream encounter. My visitor was invisible but he made his presence known by opening a door in a room that I recognised as being at my home when I was a child. I could sense that the visitor was a man and he mysteriously thanked me for "sending him the chocolates." Was he implying that I'd done him a favour somehow? He moved towards me; I was sitting on a sofa and I felt two invisible hands clasp me around my ankles, as if to pull me off the seat. "I can help you, you know," he said.

Upon awaking I asked Charlotte whether this new arrival was actually a friend. Like hell, he was! I realised this straight away. In the nights that followed I received further messages from my visitor, although these were rather less cordial. After a few more of these encounters, I realised there was going to be trouble and Charlotte agreed.

On Christmas Eve, Tom and I went out for a drink and I told him about my latest experiences and that there may be trouble ahead. Around midnight, I lay in bed reading a magazine and Tom was sound asleep in the next room. Suddenly, I heard the ominous sound of a footstep on the bottom step of the stairs. I was gripped with alarm, and upon asking Charlotte if it was whom I thought it to be, my suspicions were confirmed. For God's sake, had he actually come into the house? Was he a poltergeist? "I'm afraid so," she replied. And once more I heard the stairs creak, as if he too could hear my thoughts.

Suddenly, in my mind's eye I saw an image of what he looked like, appearing as a photographic negative of his overall appearance: a scrawny, gangly-looking figure, dressed in eighteenth century costume. The legs were abnormally bowed and after a while I realised he had had rickets when he was on the Earth. In all, I got the impression his life had been a harsh one and it didn't surprise me that he had preferred to be invisible before. I tried knocking the wall to wake Tom, but to no avail as he was in a deep sleep. This was unusual. I was now becoming rather panicky, especially as I could hear the floorboards creaking on the landing outside my bedroom door, just a few feet away from my bed in fact. The door was wide open and it looked out onto the landing, although I couldn't actually see anything, just the shadowy darkness. Charlotte assured me he wouldn't come any nearer, although this took some accepting. However, I soon found that she was right. I desperately wanted to be with Tom, although at first Charlotte told me it would be unsafe to go onto the landing. A while later she gave me the go-ahead, but by this time I was too afraid to leave my room – and Tom was still fast asleep.

Time passed and somehow, although God knows how, I began to settle. As I put my head on the pillow, I received pleasant images of what appeared to be Princess Diana looking after some children in a nursery. But shortly I found them being intercepted by images of death in black and white, showing valleys of skulls followed by death masks making obscene gestures. The latter I knew were from my unwelcome visitor. Amid this ordeal I passed into sleep at some stage and to my knowledge I was undisturbed.

Later on, in the welcome light of day, I told Tom about what had happened earlier at that ungodly hour. It was the worst Christmas morning ever. He made plans to get rid of the intruder in the early hours of the next morning, which revealed a facet of him I didn't know about – he was a dark horse, was Tom. I was reassured by Charlotte to have faith, that Tom was capable of dealing with this. For the rest of the day I lived in the disturbing knowledge that our intruder was on the first flight of stairs, watching and waiting. However, there was no danger from him in the daylight hours and to some degree we ignored his presence by watching the Christmas programmes on television.

Around mid-afternoon I could sense spirit drawing closer to me. I felt a distinct chill around me that even sitting close to the heating wouldn't ease. I wasn't harmed in any way though. It came to me that during his time on Earth our intruder had taken orders, not given them, and that he was born into the servile classes. Following this it came through that he was the base-born son of a lord: that he was Ruth's second child by Charles Townshend. If he is anything to go by, they were a horrible family; you can learn more about this in Chapter 8. It transpired that I was being visited by both Charlotte and the intruder at that time.

At the third hour of the next morning, Tom and I ascended the stairs (we'd been up watching television until then). Again, I felt a distinct chill on the first flight of steps as we made our way, although there was no harm. Tom claimed that this was the best time to per-form the task since there is an increase in 'cosmic energies' now. I lay down near Tom and anxiously watched him go to sleep; very soon his breathing became laboured, as if he were in some kind of fight, and I knew his spirit was outside on the landing confronting our intruder. After about ten minutes of this, Tom returned to consciousness and told me that he had had some success in making the fiend retreat, at least for now. It was a gruelling ordeal but thankfully he was none the worse for it. He told me that the intruder was around his mid-twenties when he died, although he looked a good deal older, adding that he looked gangly and spider-like. This confirmed what I'd been shown.

I felt an acute sense of guilt, sorely regretting that I had this ability to communicate with spirit. But Tom supported me by saying that he would be there for me and I drew strength from this amidst what seemed a disaster at the time. Still, I knew that the ordeal was not over and furthermore it would be a long time before it was.

Ready for Freddy?

The following day there was another incident while we were at a petrol station. This happened during the daytime, which made it even more unnerving. I was sitting in the car while Tom was filling up and suddenly I became aware of an invisible presence on the back seat. It was you-know-who. I screamed and jumped out, whereupon Tom sternly told me to take control of myself and not to let him succeed in distracting me as there was a real danger of this. We got into the car and drove off, regardless of whether there was anyone else in with us or not. I don't think he hung about when Tom returned, actually.

We didn't need to watch any scary films – we were having our own Nightmare on Elm Street. In fact our whole lives took on a sense of being surreal. I turned over the events of the last few days and tried to come to terms with it. To think, I had an enemy on 'the other side' from all that time ago who still bore hatred towards me for whatever happened then and, furthermore, wanted to destroy me in this life too. At first I thought that maybe his harsh life had had a bearing on it but no, I found out later that he would have been evil regardless of that. So no sympathy, please. Also I was to find that he hated me for what I am destined to do in this life. My guess is that he must have spent many lifetimes as an evil-doer, as I learned from Charlotte that he is 'in the spirit world to stay'. This means that he came from what is referred to in the Bible as the place called She'ol – a place of darkness and punishment cut off from life and from God, whose inhabitants are the 'shades'. Yes indeed, there really is such a place. I could tell that Charlotte found this rather difficult to put across.

Night-time rolled in and upon retiring to bed we became aware that once more he had to be dealt with. I sensed that this time he had enlisted support from other fiends. More disturbing images of Death Valley came through my mind's eye, whole valleys made up of skulls in black and white. He was showing me where he'd come from, no doubt. I also saw strident images of a devil lashing its tail. This time I felt I should take a stand in all this: I wanted to fight as well, but Charlotte's reaction was discouraging. So that night we went to sleep with the disturbing knowledge that there was a gang of evil spirits waiting for us on the landing outside our bedroom!

When I crossed over into sleep, I found myself lying on the bed dressed in chainmail armour with a white tunic bearing the symbol of a red cross, as if I were a Templar Knight in the Holy Wars. Very appropriate. I felt myself being lifted up by some invisible forces and whirled around, then I awoke. Tom told me that he had also found himself wearing a chainmail gauntlet on his right hand and was aware of being surrounded by a mob of low-life characters. When 'Rickets' had come to the fore as the ringleader, Tom had hit him hard in the face, knocking him to the ground senseless. He then got up and made a hearty breakfast, recounting the scene in more detail. "He went down like a ninepin and after that the rest of the buggers dispersed." Tom was very pleased with himself about this, crowing that it would be "a long time before that shit gets back up again."

And so it was. This feat had got our tormenter out of the house, although it was quite a few weeks before I could accept that he had gone since it was not something I was accustomed to although it was evident that Tom was no stranger to it. Even so, it had been a harrowing time for us both. During this period I went through a spell of what they call anxiety disorder, waking in the mornings with a knot-like feeling in my stomach, being off my food for a while and drinking too much alcohol. Most of all, I didn't feel safe and felt I could be revisited at any time, so I lived in fear and dread, both consciously and subconsciously.

Ship ahoy

It was New Year's Eve. As I lay resting alone, vainly trying to free my mind of the trauma, I unexpectedly received a visit from James 'Partly' Murray. This was a rare pleasure lately as he hadn't made any contact for a while now. My eyes were closed when suddenly the image of a large galleon came into view; I could clearly see it approaching from across the high sea, drawing nearer and nearer. Following this I beheld a close-up, head and shoulders image of him and he drew attention to his rather imposing-looking hat of military office, similar to that worn by Napoleon Bonaparte. It gave me the impression that he wished to portray himself as he was when he was a military commander, for some reason.

Subsequently, he showed himself as a fatherly figure, although this was not as well defined, and I could make out that he was warmly embracing some young children. They all appeared in clothes of that period and the general feeling of the scene was warm and convivial, rather like Santa in his grotto. Actually he was showing me his own children of those times and he rather touchingly conveyed that he loved them dearly. After a while, I realised that he was trying to tell me that he could be likewise towards me – a father figure – whereupon I asked if he could take the edge off the anxiety that was searing through me. He replied that he could. The next thing I knew was that a wonderful calming sensation began flowing through me, for which I was extremely grateful and felt much revived by.

Then a few minutes later, just a stone's throw away, I heard the bottom stairs begin to creak with dreadful familiarity… I went deathly quiet, but was relieved to find that it was James. I hadn't realised he had drawn in quite that close. I flew into a fit of anger, totally appalled that he would subject me to this. Just what were his intentions? I was soon to find, though, that it was actually part of his plan to harden me to my ordeal: it's not just evil spirits who come into your house and make noises.

So in January, 1999, I resumed the routine of my normal job. It was a welcome break after spending such a horrendous Christmas. To see me about performing my daily duties, no-one would have guessed what I'd been through, so outwardly all appeared fine. It made me wonder how many more people experience similar things, as I couldn't believe we were unique by any means.

I started again to become sensitive to energies surrounding me, especially negative ones. When out shopping, I would feel the bad energy emitted from some videos on sale in a shop we had started going to; they were sick and I gave them a wide berth. At home, I became aware of dust and clutter in some rooms and felt the release of positive energy as I cleared it. These were psychic energy centres in the house. The most memorable of these clearings related to some African masks I had in my bedroom, which I suddenly realised to be voodoo masks. They had unknowingly been a gift from my father who'd been on holiday in Gran Canaria about nine years before. It was quite a relief for both of us when these were disposed of, although the evil spirits connected with them had a final fling the night before they went. I stayed awake all night though I was still aware of them. Tom encountered them during his sleep. We found ourselves being skirmished by the spirits of black native African children; Tom experienced it worse, seeing a group of nasty, gremlin-like spirits coming at us like gnats. I took all the masks to the local refuse tip around ten a.m. the following morning. It had to be done before noon as there is a cosmic energy shift at this hour, apparently and they would have been stronger by then. Tom stayed at home, although he told me that he had felt a weight lift from him as I threw them into the skip.

Speaking of partings, it was one night around the second week of this month that I became aware of James leaving. At first, it felt like it was for good, but afterwards I gathered that it was for something like six months. There was some 'catching up' he had to do, or something like that. Whatever it was, I recall bidding him an emotional au revoir and wished him every success with what he had to do. Early the following morning at around six a.m. he was 'replaced', if you can call it that, by a woman whom I'd not known before although I was to learn that she'd always been around. She was Gertrude, a member of the famous Pelham family of the eighteenth century and a daughter of the parliamentary minister Henry Pelham.

I was to find that she is a resolute, down-to-earth type. The term 'matron' springs to mind and sums her up rather well. Sometimes, though, she was like an elder sister while at other times she was a mentor, advising me to keep focused on the positive aspects of a situation, on the light rather than the darkness. This is an important aspect of life. During the time we had together, I found that I was a good channel for giving healing energy. There were frequent occasions on which I sent out absent healing to those in need and, when we did this together, she always appeared as a housewife about her daily chores in a country cottage of the period she had lived in.

The healing energy streamed outwards through what appeared as ribbons of colour, sometimes as a sheer veil of colour and at other times as a block of colour that melted into blackness, like fat in a frying pan. Amidst these colours I could see her long skirts bustling about as she went about the tasks. In the main, these appeared as apparently mundane household chores: sweeping up with a besom broom, cooking meals and dishing them up, or sometimes she sat spinning at her wheel. Occasionally she even went outside to feed some geese. What did any of this signify – is giving healing like doing housework, then? I wondered. Well yes, it is rather. Whatever, I know she was a grafter during these sessions and that her intentions were always for the highest and greatest good.

I know that our efforts did help Tom for a time with the arthritis in his knees. They also helped ease the suffering of his poor dog, who developed cancer later that year. Months before we even knew about Whiskey's illness, sometimes I saw healing energy being 'fed' to the figure of a dog that resembled him. My attentions were focused on

Tom at the time so I thought no more of it. As time went by, it all went to prove to me that the objectives of a good spirit should not be doubted, however strange they may seem to begin with. Indeed they do move in mysterious ways. Sometimes, some of us are just allowed a glimpse of 'the big picture'.

One of the enviable qualities that Gertrude possessed was that of never giving in. Where there is love, faith and a desire to change for the better, there is always hope. When I felt her presence amidst the turmoil that later ensued during the time she was with me, there was no doubt that she belonged to the light, devoted to helping out in a crisis.

A crusade of terror

'Rickets' again made himself known quite frequently for a time too, although from then on it was only in dream encounters, which was bad enough. Needless to say these were always nightmarish. (Just for the record, I'm almost certain it was he whom Liz had encountered in the disturbing scene of the Madam gargling up blood. This is because I have discovered that spirit can appear in any form they wish to, and I'm sure he was trying to deter her from looking into it any further.)

There was little truth in the things he put across. However, there was one instance in the early hours of January morning when we had a disquieting message from him. He vividly conveyed a dark and grue-some scene, in which a man had his head cleaved and his body thrown into a river. He even went into detail of how the corpse decomposed in the water. We believe this is how he actually met his own end. In other scenes he showed us that he had been blackmailing George over the murder incident and, shall we say, went just a bit too far. So George had him discreetly disposed of one night, no doubt as a deterrent to other blackmailers. My guess is that this would explain why Mistress Stringer only made one attempt.

I suppose he had always held a bit of a grudge ever since really, especially considering what he is. Over the next three years or so, the persecution we both endured became terrible and it pushed us both to the very edge since never before had either of us experienced evil quite like this. I was regularly menaced with hate messages. Once he chillingly conveyed that I would be "unhinged by clairvoyance" and that he could "cut my life short". There were also times when he acquired the help of other fiends to give us similar messages and quite often I was menaced by horrific attacks during my sleep. At other times I felt him draining my energy during the day when I was at work. When he was not behaving like a thug, I was sickened by the atrocity of his obscenities. Tom experienced similar things, although he could cope better than me.

The most disturbing of all his threats was that on some mornings I would awake with the sensation that there were tender lumps in my breasts. There was much publicity in the media about cancer research at the time, particularly breast cancer, and this only pumped up the scare volume, so to speak. Tom told me that 'Rickets' had done this by autosuggestion to my subconscious during my sleep. These feelings remained with me for days at a time, sometimes running into weeks, and caused me much distress as they were so real. Actually, there was nothing really there. At other times I would get feverish pains in my head and was unable to concentrate clearly. I even had memory loss, as if I were developing dementia.

Thankfully, I found that I was able to dispel the effects of these negative suggestions by meditating on positive thoughts. It was not easy to start with as I had to overcome my fear, which only fed the curse. Fear emits a low vibrational energy that evil entities feed off so wherever possible they induce this state in humanity to achieve their purpose. The brain is like a transmitter and a receiving set in one. I came to learn of the psychic effect of the power of thought in our material lives.

This was working, because within a short time I had another dream encounter with him but this time I pushed him through the door of a washing machine and turned it on to full spin. I must have thought he needed a good clean. Eventually he emerged from it looking weak and anaemic. I was able to walk away from him and began climbing a steep, narrow stairway, although this was a gruelling task. Looking up, I could see an interview room at the top and there was a woman in a suit waiting in a doorway. She had no idea of what I'd been through earlier. I then awoke.

In July of that year I was pleased to know of James's return. We were on a day trip to the seaside and I became aware that he was nearby while I was paddling in the water – yes, we did have some nice times amid all the trouble. He put himself across as being like a school Headmaster, someone with influence. It seems that while he was away he had evolved somewhat.

I told the birds to come to the edge of the cliff. "No, we are afraid," the birds cried. Finally the birds came. I pushed. And they flew.

In April of the new millennium he collaborated with Tom to administer to me a 'programme' he had arranged which would release me from the persecution for good, should I complete it. As it happened, this carried on until August of the following year, so it was no fast track antidote by any means. It was a time of much self-assessment and reform, a weeding out of the nasty aspects of me, to put it plainly; much of this was a legacy from George and the reasons why he had to be reincarnated. How I grew to detest what he had been. In a few instances I had to figure out for myself where I was in the wrong and indeed I often felt lost and hopeless, but it was all par for the course. As James said to me on a number of occasions, "The purest ore comes from the hottest furnace." It was a gruelling time. There was actually a song that came out in the charts then that conveyed pretty well how I felt, called Never Ever by All Saints; the context was different and I was more scared than sad, but apart from that the lyrics were spot on.

One of the most important things I learned was to stay positive in adversity, especially when other people were not. I was put into a number of situations where I had to infuse the negative with positive. On reflection, they reminded me a bit of the trials faced by the contestants in 'I'm A Celebrity, Get Me Out Of Here'! Or perhaps 'Hell's Kitchen' would be more fitting. It's true that metaphorically this is a very important aspect of life generally.

It is said that "Most of the problems on this Earth are caused by the weakness of good, rather than the strength of evil." By making my own progress I found that I was able to overcome the power of that evil spirit and to stop the devastating harm he was causing in my life. In short, good had to triumph over evil. "Prove as strong," I kept being told. Like so many things on this Earth, more harm has been done by weak people than by wicked people.

But can leopards change their spots? There was a rather chilling meeting I had with 'Rickets' at the start of this programme, among those I will never forget. I found myself sitting with him in the living room of my childhood home. I had a clear impression of his appearance being that of a young man with short red hair and a beard. Sitting nearby with folded arms, he referred to the reform that I was undergoing. It seemed that there had been some kind of contract drawn up that would release me from his attack, subject to me living up to the requirements.

"So, you have these good intentions, but will you keep to them?" he wanted to know. I replied that I would. With a cynical smile he nodded his head, saying, "That's good – because if you don't, there'll be more of this…" and, reaching over, he prodded me at a spot between my shoulder blades. I awoke with an odd sensation running down my left arm, as if I had a trapped nerve, and a wave of dread swept over me like a tsunami. Getting a grip, I later steeled myself to rise to the challenge.

Just for the record, I'll mention another such meeting later in which I had a moment of triumph; indeed, I had been living up to my word. Once again I found myself in a room with him, although this time there was no conversation; as my spirit began to rise above him, ascending well out of his reach, he tried to do likewise but couldn't. Upon awaking, my last memory was of him looking up at me in defeat. I was beating him. He couldn't touch me. Yet more, I needed to do more.

In the least likely place

Yes, 'more' seemed to be the catch-word at this stage. Besides my starting on 'The Programme', there was another noteworthy event in the month of April. At long last we were able to deduce where Ruth Hartwell had got married. I say 'deduce' because there's no surviving record of the marriage, which had been bugging me for ages. And it turned out to be where I wouldn't have thought of looking.

Our researcher wrote with much enthusiasm about another Ruth she had found, this time with the surname Barnes, who was working on the Raynham estate at the appropriate time. She considers Ruth Barnes as a more suitable candidate for being a mistress. She first appears in December, 1746, almost at the same time that Ruth Hartwell was mentioned, in June of the same year. Since Ruth was an unusual Christian name then, the researcher wondered whether they were the same person. I would say so. She thinks it possible that Ruth and Benjamin Dimont were married in London, as household accounts mention frequent visits to the Townshend's London house. She found the first mention of Ruth Dimont in June, 1751, as a housemaid. There is a reference to 'Ruth Barnes' later, in September, but this might have been a memory lapse of whoever wrote the accounts.

The family went to London between October, 1751, and August, 1752, and the servants' names appear again at Raynham in April, 1752. There's no Ruth, but Elizabeth Walker appears for the first time as a housemaid. By this time Ruth had had a baby, Elizabeth, born in 1751, so it all seems to make sense. I suspect that she had other offspring who are untraceable since it was the way of things for a lot of women in those days, that they had several children.

We came upon another interesting snippet of information in August of that year when looking at various maps and documents. This was that the Stringers, the Walkers and the Goodwins were all in occupation in the parish of Raynham for possibly over two hundred years. In that case, it occurred to me that they could have had branches in several other places, including, significantly, Ireland.

Back in the saddle

Around mid-May we made contact with Liz again. She had been discharged from hospital and had also separated from her boyfriend and we were able to meet up again a few times. As we spoke over the `phone once, she started visualising a scene where she could see herself in a room by a fire with a cooking pot hanging over it, in a past era. Next she knew that she was in the company of a soldier in this room and that she was bent over a table with her skirts over her head, laughing. He was standing behind her with his hands planted either side of her on the table… I suspected the entire regiment was queuing up outside! I might have known she would recall something like that; it was good for a laugh, though, which heaven knows I needed.

Another time when I met with her, she told me that she had been involved with a publican after she and George had parted company. It was a Moll Flanders scenario, where she had used her charms to get with him. When I think of it, much of her life story could have come out of the pages of that book. She went on to describe a gory scene which sounded as if she'd had a primitive abortion performed on her with a knitting needle. I sent her some healing one night, in which I visualised water gushing from a fountain, but it transformed into gin pouring from a bottle; next I saw images of Lolita with heart-shaped sunglasses, seductively sucking on an ice lolly. Yes, it made sense that this was why she needed healing.

Of all these insights, the most noteworthy were her revelations about George and Benjamin as they grew up. Sadly there was much acrimony between them: George frequently made his half-brother feel inadequate and not up to par with the rest of the Townshend family. Well, he just wasn't as bright as they were for one thing since he had failed most of his schooling.

Liz and I went out one evening to the service at the local Christian Spiritualist church where she lived. Previously, I had received much counselling there during the episodes with Rickets, about protection especially. Having had an encounter with him themselves, they knew what I was up against. They also supported the fact that Tom and I are soulmates. That evening, it so happened that I received a message through the medium, addressing some poignant former life issues between Tom and myself which had carried over into this life.

Afterwards, Liz was prompted to add that there had been plots between Benjamin and her former self actually to kill George. He would often speak with her in confidence about 'the damned Townshends' and how he keenly wished to be rid of his half-brother. She continued that for the main part he kept his feelings secret and presented a sly, ingratiating mask to everyone else. Intrigue upon intrigue. This story was becoming like a soap opera. Upon relaying Liz's insight to Tom, I found that it wasn't news to him at all. I was taken aback. It turned out that Tom had kept this under wraps for a long time. He added that the plots were ultimately dropped because she had wanted too large a cut of the blood money, which would have come from Benjamin's inheritance – apparently he stood to gain a large portion of George's estate in the event of him dying beforehand.

Since then, however, I have learned that illegitimate offspring were not included in family inheritance unless there were a special trust fund set up. So I assume this applied in this case. In fact, I clearly recall Tom remarking this upon telling him about the blackmail money she had acquired following the murder. Could this also have a bearing on what Liz had referred to as her 'betrayal' in the incident at Wall? Of course, I had to consult Gertrude about this and she affirmed that everything that had come to light was correct… It is such a tragedy that George was like that towards Benjamin.

7

Let's Go Exploring

It was now high time for us to go exploring some more of the places connected with our story. So in September of 2000, and in January and February of the year following, we took a few holidays to southern Ireland and the Norfolk coast. Indeed, we came upon more pieces of the jigsaw, as we had anticipated we would; I had a few pretty memorable experiences in Norfolk, which were related to what had happened in George's life and in connection with smuggling, believe it or not. Now's the time when I tell in more detail what this was about. There's also a confirmation at Clonakilty in Ireland, not forgetting an unexpected meeting with my grandfather, which stirred up a few things.

In the last week of September we embarked on our long anticipated expedition to Ireland. It was our first ever trip to 'the Emerald Isle' and we were full of excitement, both as researchers and as holiday makers. Catching the ferry at Pembroke Dock, we landed at Rosslare around 7 p.m. and thereon drove as far as Wexford, where we found lodgings for the night. The following morning we headed for the city of Cork via Waterford County, and around midday we booked in at an exclusive guest house at Tivoli, which is just a mile out of the city. From there we journeyed south to the coast at Castletownshend via Bandon, Clonakilty and Skibbereen. The roads became noticeably rougher at

Bandon and this alone made us feel like we were taking a trip back in time. At any minute, we half expected to encounter a coach and horses.

Upon reaching the outskirts of Clonakilty, Tom suddenly noticed a statue of the Virgin Mary. It drew him so much that he immediately about-turned to get a closer look. He must have picked up a vibration from it as I didn't even see it myself. It transpired that this was the main feature of the gardens of a home run by the Holy Sisters. When we eventually got to see the Sister in charge we learned that the place dated back as far as the eighteenth century and from its earliest beginnings had been a respite for unmarried mothers. In that instant, Tom's intuition was verified. For me it was like a prophesy enacting itself: I had understood Charlotte correctly. Indeed this had been the place of refuge that Liz had envisaged Mistress Stringer seeking on that inclement eventide all those years ago. I couldn't help feeling a strange twinge of guilt in the presence of this place, considering George's part in this, though I suppose there was really no need since I'm neither a man nor part of the nobility any more.

In her very broad Irish accent, the Sister also told us of another such place at Skibbereen. Nowadays, this is a hospital that she said may have records dating back to that specific time, as they held none there. This was a pity but came as no surprise really. With much gratitude we thanked her for her help and continued on our way. As we passed Clonakilty I had more guilty feelings as I imagined the doorway Mistress Stringer had stood in two and a half centuries ago. I thought of the desperate poverty she had been part of and also the neglect she had suffered. Despite her faults, the blame here rested on George, and passing by the place seemed to emphasise this disagreeable fact.

The road to Skibbereen is long and winding, approximately twenty miles from Clonakilty and cutting through a hilly landscape. As we meandered in and out, it became obvious why Liz had thought she had travelled fifty miles or more. But it's unlikely she made this journey on foot, as she had said, although we could appreciate why it felt like that. Tom suggested that she probably begged a lift on the back of a trader's cart along the way. I had another twinge of regret, but it was pointless as it was happening nearly three centuries too late.

The scenery was very pleasant though, and it served well to divert my thoughts from the significance here.

Upon arriving at Skibbereen we made enquiries at the said hospital, only to find that there are no surviving records there either, although they did recommend a local historian who was the owner of the main hotel in Skibbereen. Upon leaving, Tom had a feeling that Mistress Stringer had initially called here but found no room at the inn, so to speak. While we were there we called in at the local library asking about parish records and we were given the address of the local priest. But it was late in the afternoon by then and Tom felt in need of a rest, so we found the hotel and made enquiries at the bar as to the availability of the proprietor. He was going to be in the next day. So after a drink or two we rounded the trip off by heading for Castletownshend, with a view to spending about half an hour or so checking out the place where it had all started.

Situated about a mile from Skibbereen, Castletownshend is indeed a very small coastal village. "A small corner of a county" sums it up well. Upon arriving we found it consisted quite simply of a narrow cobbled street leading down a steep gradient towards a small harbour. Both sides were lined with a row of quaint terraced houses and nestling about midway on the right-hand side going down was a public house called 'Mary Ann's', which seemed to draw me for some reason. Tom passed it by on this occasion as he really didn't want to spend long here and he'd had enough to drink by then in any case! The main features of the village are the manor house, the castle and the church, the latter being prominently perched on top of a steep hill with a stairway of stone steps ascending to it, giving it a very gothic feel. Just the sort of place to have bats in the belfry and spooks in the crypt. Apart from that there was nothing else that held any interest, but on leaving I did sense an energy as we drove past the manor house.

The eccentric genealogist

The next day we met the owner of the hotel at Skibbereen and he referred us to George Salter Townshend, the proprietor of the local bus service, who lived in the house opposite to Mary Ann's at Castletownshend.

I just knew that place had some significance. He is a member of the Irish Townshends who lives by himself while the rest of his family live at the manor. We were told that he was our most likely bet in matters such as reincarnation since he is a medium, therefore making it rather more his field.

By chance we did find him at home but had to bide our time for an hour, so we went across the road. I bought a large glass of red wine to give him as an icebreaker when the time came. We found him a rather talkative sort who spoke much about his family and their academic successes – not neglecting to mention his own. He had an avid interest in genealogy, so much so that in fact he had written a book about a genealogical system he had devised, in which he claimed that he could prove that everyone in the world is interrelated... A bit of an eccentric, we felt, but maybe just the person we needed. Anyway, I suppose some would say that we were pretty eccentric too.

Time passed well in his congenial company and at length I told him about our project. "Yes, actually there was a murder in that family around that time," he admitted. This sounded rather encouraging at first, but I was to find later that he was probably referring to the well documented murder that happened between two sons of the First Marquis. Insanity was the issue there. Well, what we wanted was to hear tell of another murder by their father at an earlier date, where temporary insanity was also the issue.

We told him that we wanted to find evidence of the Barnes and Stringer families in these parts, so Salter gave us a contact number for the local Protestant vicar for access to the parish records. "See how you get on with that first of all, and if you have no luck you can call back and we can try tracing the families through my genealogical system." Later that evening we did give the vicar a call, only to find that all Irish parish records were submitted to the National Library in Dublin and were later destroyed in the famous Four Courts Fire of 1922. Why didn't Salter know this? A later search around the churchyard at Castletownshend proved unfruitful too.

Upon arriving at Salter's house the following day, he cordially invited us in. "I trust," Tom joked, "that you've returned the glass to

90

the pub by now." "Of course not, where d'ye think I get all my glasses from?" Salter retorted. He expressed surprise at the outcome of our enquiries but offered his alternative nonetheless. He asked us to run the plot by him again and once more I told him about the murder. At this point he became reticent, saying dismissively that "We really needed to be looking the other side of the water, because, quite simply he didn't live over here." I agreed, but countered that the English Townshends often visited these parts and had much to do with the local folk. He found this quite acceptable and agreed to help so we exchanged contact details. But nothing came of it so it seems that his genealogical system was not as good as he had made it out to be.

From here we put the research aside and continued on our sight-seeing holiday, heading north to Killarney. Now, the landscape here truly is memorable; to me, it looked like a smaller version of the Grand Canyon in green.

Hello Gramps

The next day we set off on our return journey to England. Around 7 p.m. we arrived at Rosslare to catch the boat and decided to spend the next couple of hours driving around the surrounding area before boarding the ferry. We came upon a place called Carne Beach, which is near to Tagoat, and stopping off here I went for a walk along the beach by myself for something like an hour. To me at that time it was the most magical beach I'd ever seen. Bathed in the shimmering evening sunlight of late summer, it exuded a special charisma. The cold wind blew in from the sea and I gazed about me taking in the beach scene reminiscent of the film 'Ryan's Daughter'. While sitting in the dunes, I could sense the presence of spirit drawing near. I knew that it was a man, but there was no threat as by his aura I could sense he was a good man. At first I thought it was someone from our former lives but I soon realised that it was my grandfather on my mother's side. I never knew him as he'd passed before I was born, but I'd heard him mentioned a few times when I was a child; a good sort indeed. It seemed that his father was from Ireland, though not he himself, and I felt there was some connection to Carne Beach but didn't know quite what. Thinking about it, this is quite fitting actually.

This was quite an unexpected pleasure, although it was strange to be with a member of my family whom I'd never known. Perhaps this is why I thought of 'Ryan's Daughter'? What's more, I was aware that he remained with me until we arrived safely back at our home in Telford the following morning; in retrospect, it seemed that he had also come to protect us during our return. More than anything, it made me realise that I must make contact with my mother again.

In the latter part of October my thoughts once more turned to Mistress Stringer. Could I get away from her? I considered what Liz had told me about the publican and I could not resist asking James about it. I was to find that he wasn't a publican exactly, but something similar, and she wasn't married to him either. Illicit dealings of some sort had a bearing here too. What seemed more important was that later she was also involved with a fisherman at a place called Caister-on-Sea in Norfolk. It was here that she also met her end.

So Tom and I concluded that to wind up our research we must pay a visit to Norfolk, to sort this out. The elusive cave and the shady world of smuggling was coming to the fore also in connection with this and Tom's feeling now was that Norfolk would be the place to find it.

The lawless coast

On the 11th of January, 2000, we set off on our much anticipated venture to Norfolk in search of the mysterious cave Tom knew about. He had a gut feeling that we'd find it at Lowestoft, although our researcher gave us a number of likely places along this coastal region. We arrived at Norwich around mid-afternoon and took lodgings at a place called Riverside on the outskirts of the city. The landlady suggested the most likely place to explore would be Cromer, so we decided to start our search from this port of call, just to exclude any doubts from our minds. I'm pleased to say that the day's findings bore fruit, making the trip well worth it – despite there being an unpleasant encounter along the way. But we were used to that by now.

At Cromer, Tom headed first to the nearest car wash, as our new car needed a good clean after making the journey through rural Norfolk. While he did this, I went for a walk around and I experienced another of my 'twilight zone' moments, recognising the main street of the town from a spirit message I had received just a few days before Christmas. There was a distinctive atmosphere to the place that I also picked up on. As it happens, this is characteristic of the Norfolk coast and I found it uncanny to be physically visiting the place now.

Looking back, I think Cromer must have had significance for George, although not for Benjamin it seems, as Tom felt no connection at all. We continued walking together along the pier and asked a local man passing by if he knew of any caves in the cliffs. He replied with certainty that there were none, but I still couldn't shake the feeling that this place had something. From here we drove along the coast road, keeping our senses open, but to no avail. Our next stop was Caister-on-Sea, allegedly Mistress Stringer's place of marriage. We spent a short time there but got no such vibrations; Tom quipped that it was not surprising really – she was not the sort to get married.

We continued journeying south and upon reaching Great Yarmouth I suddenly became aware that I was under 'psychic attack', which grew worse as we approached Lowestoft. After a while, I began to feel rather drained of energy and we had to stop off in Lowestoft to recharge my battery. We didn't know what it was about, nor whom it was from, but we felt that smuggling had a bearing on it. The attack subsided after we'd parked up at the first available pub, but I was still in need of recharging.

After a Guinness for sustenance and a greatly revived morale, we set off for the harbour where we stood on the jetty at the entrance and both felt an energy strongly connected to our quest. Tom especially felt that our cave was nearby, but trying to pinpoint it proved to be a drain on both of us. Undeterred, Tom asked a couple who were passing by if they knew of such a cave, whereupon we learned there had been one until fairly recently, but it had been demolished to make way for commercial developments. There had been boats moored on the beach in front of it, just as Tom had seen in his previous visit here in August, 1996. We had finally found the cave, or at least where it had been.

Whether or not that cave dated back to the eighteenth century, we can't say, but it doesn't really matter. That it was at a place with a long history of smuggling was enough and we were content with our discovery here. Thus we made our return trip to Norwich in the dimming light of that cold January day of the new millennium, with keen intent to recharge ourselves for whatever the next day would bring.

For further information about smuggling in eighteenth century Britain, there is 'The Lawless Coast' by Neil Homes. Published eight years after we made these trips, it gives a detailed account of smuggling in olden days and I only wish this book had been around when we were doing our research! It particularly took my interest that by 1780 smuggling had reached unprecedented heights in Britain and in north Norfolk especially. It is also significant that Overstrand, which is situated a mile down the road from Cromer, is among the villages with this association. The relevance of this village to our story will become clear a little further on. Yes, Homes' book certainly clarifies some of the experiences I had in those parts.

Just as a postscript to all of this, I should mention that my mysterious attacker had been the unsavoury character whom Tom had met at the initial cave visit. I came to find that he was the father of 'Rickets' – it certainly made sense.

Feeling much better, the following morning we set off on our final visit, heading for Fakenham, to fulfil another long-awaited desire to visit Raynham Hall. This was the jewel in the crown of the trip, as we saw it. We had planned to take the main road out of Norwich; however, by a twist of fate it happened that we took the scenic route. After spending quite a long time meandering around the labyrinth that is rural Norfolk, we eventually came upon a quaint, picturesque village called Reepham. It was like reaching the centre of a maze, quite in character. We headed for the local pub, namely 'The King's Arms', and upon entering Tom felt some familiar and rather strong energy. The hour was late morning and there was only one other customer at the bar. On reflection, this had been the scenario before when we were about to make a random discovery.

We spent a happy hour chatting with the local man and I asked if he knew of any caves on the coastline, whereupon he told of one just below Cromer at a place called Overstrand (see above). To me this was very interesting, although Tom firmly declined to visit it this time and I had to agree as we had suffered enough of an ordeal at Lowestoft for one outing, especially as we were on holiday.

When we finally got to Fakenham we felt, as we had expected, a mutual familiarity with the place. Tom took a rest, the arthritis in his knees starting to play up by then, so I went for a walk by myself. Every turn of every street had something about it. The most memorable thing for me was the ancient church in the centre of town, which towered over the place in a most imposing way, unlike any I'd seen before. We noticed that this is characteristic of all the old churches that loom on the flat Norfolk landscape. And at this time of year they all emit a grim air of foreboding, like something out of 'The Omen'. I don't think this was a favourite place of George's.

From here we finished off our trip by heading to Raynham Hall, filled with great expectation. As we progressed down the long driveway we could picture ourselves riding along it on horseback in our former lives. Yes, there was a familiar feeling along this stretch of road. But strangely, the Hall is where the familiarity ended; as we sat on the drive outside the house, neither of us could sense anything in particular and it made us wonder if we had spent much time there at all formerly. It was an anti-climax really, rather like Castletownshend. The setting was pleasant enough though, and we could vaguely sense some familiarity with that.

Raynham Hall, Norfolk
Photo © the author

I got the feeling that it was meant that we should make that detour to Reepham, so we would come to know about the cave at Overstrand, of course. It was a better fish to fry, perhaps, but not on this trip unfortunately so we made our journey home. In the last few days of the month the feeling re-emerged that George had been involved in smuggling at some stage, probably after his governorship of Ireland during which he ran up huge debts leaving him considerably short of money. It would also account for Tom's indifference to Cromer, simply because Benjamin had been a long time dead by then. But I was now very keen to visit Overstrand, as I was becoming certain we would find something there. Tom agreed and we made plans to return in early February.

Thus we embarked on our second visit to Norfolk, intent on tying up the loose ends that remained tantalisingly unanswered. Around late afternoon we arrived at Cromer and booked in at a seafront hotel called 'The Cliftonville'. More than pleased with our lodgings, we then set off for Overstrand, which lies about a mile to the south along the coast road. We found that it is a small village, looking desolate. Everything was closed at this time of year and even the inhabitants seemed to be in hibernation. Looking about us, we noticed that most of the properties were run down and apt to send chills through the onlooker, especially in this fading light.

We walked to a point on the clifftop nearest to the tourist car park. This is a vantage spot where one can get a panoramic view of the sea. The whole place emitted an eerie atmosphere, emphasised by the haunting sound of the wind rattling through the fishing boats moored up in a compound nearby. After spending about a quarter of an hour milling around this lonely spot, we came upon two local lads. They were fishermen, not surprisingly. Yes, they knew of a tunnel positioned just beneath the point where we had first stood overlooking the sea. They went on to tell us that it had been filled in years ago to prevent subsidence, and that it ran to what used to be an inn, situated about one hundred yards inland where nowadays a private conference centre stands. Very interestingly, they said it was thought to have been a smuggling site at one time.

So we thanked our informants for their help and set about investigating the tunnel entrance, although Tom declined to descend the steep slope to the lower promenade. So I ventured down alone, imagining for my defence that I was 'Xena, the warrior princess'. I reasoned that if I were going to suffer another psychic attack it would have happened by now, but I still wasn't taking any chances. As I reached the level of the promenade, I could easily sense that there had been smuggling going on here once upon a time. It was not quite what our friend at Reepham had described because I was expecting to find a cave. But no matter, I was satisfied with what I picked up on here so we returned to Cromer for the rest of the evening.

After an enjoyable breakfast at the hotel, next day we retraced our movements at Overstrand. Once more I walked along the promenade on the lonely beach, this time following it to the end. I looked out on the wild, grey shoreline for as far as the eye could see, and my sense of purpose diminished upon surveying what stretched before me; intuitively I knew I wouldn't find anything more here. So we continued along the coast road for a few miles further. When we reached

Trimmingham, Tom suddenly turned down Vale Road which leads to the beach. What was this about? After parking up he told me intently that I would find something of significance here. There was an air about him that was serious, also a "Don't ask, just do it" type of attitude, so without asking any further questions I did his bidding. This time I walked along the beach for quite a distance.

I began by looking for more caves but pretty soon I became aware of the distinct energy this place emitted. I became quite absorbed in this atmosphere and a strange feeling of what felt like contrition came over me; also something that felt like bereavement. Suddenly, I became more aware of the cold easterly wind which bit through me as the feeling grew. This heaviness of spirit remained for quite some time. Were these George's feelings? Tom was right, I had found something here. After milling around for what must have been an hour I solemnly returned to the car, glad of its warmth and comfort and the congenial company of my dear Tom.

From here we set off for Caister, intent on finding out more about Mistress Stringer. En route, Tom explained that upon seeing Trimmingham on a map while I was away on the promenade at Overstrand, something told him we should go there. He also knew that I would find it rather taxing, but he chose not to mention that because he knew I'd be okay despite it. It was not something he had felt comfortable about, even so.

Later, I found that Trimmingham can be linked to the time when Charlotte passed away and that George had spent much time walking along this beach grieving her loss. It also links with when he became involved with smuggling, as I had thought before we came on this trip.

Erotica

So we continued on and, still feeling pretty miserable, I took in the coastal scenery to divert my thoughts. As bleak and as eerie as that looked there was just no chance of escape I'm afraid; the way in which the churches loomed on the landscape especially made me feel like

I was on a ghost ride. Suddenly, a series of salacious visions came flooding through my mind. It was quirky, one minute I was covered in dark clouds of despondency and the next I felt like a raving nymphomaniac… This odd shift stayed with me until we reached Caister, whereupon it evaporated without a trace. I suppose it was better than feeling thoroughly miserable anyway, and my feelings did return to normal afterwards.

It came as no surprise when James told us later that this had connections with Madam Sin: we were approaching a place that links to a time when she was at her most voracious. Concupiscence springs to mind, which describes it pretty well. If she felt like that much of the time, it's no wonder to me that she spent most of her life as a whore. It was strange being able to get inside someone else's head for a while, but it certainly gives first-hand knowledge of them!

Around midday we arrived at Caister and Tom headed for the nearest available local where we happened to get chatting with members of the local lifeboat crew who, as luck would have it, were in at the time. Again we were told that there are no caves on the coast of Caister. It came as no real surprise since erosion is prevalent on the entire coast of East Anglia after all, and we realised that any such cave would have to be a ghost of what had been there formerly. So we therefore gave the beach here a miss and, as Tom needed to take it easy, I went off on my own around the salubrious town.

There appeared to be little if indeed anything left of what was there in the eighteenth century as the present day town was developed in the century after. As I strolled around the streets I realised that there was no chance of finding Madam Sin's haunts. Just for the record, I'll say that at no time during this scout around did I experience any strange feelings such as those I'd had earlier either. I suppose this was just as well really: Heaven only knows how I might have behaved had I started feeling like her again. On the last day of our trip I went strolling around Cromer once more to retrace my steps. The sights and feelings of the place were strongly familiar from the message I had had before Christmas and I found this quite enjoyable. This increased when I looked in at a seafront Bed and Breakfast property that I felt drawn to. Amazingly, its features matched those I'd seen in the dream. I was being given a tip, no doubt, that in future visits we would have to come here.

In the early afternoon we made our way back home. En route we stopped off at Fakenham and King's Lynn, neither of which bore much familiarity this time. The strongest sensations came as we passed through Whittlesey, approaching Peterborough. The houses that lined both sides of the road emitted a prominent significance of some kind. Tom mentioned that they were old army houses, if that was anything to go by; but for how long had this place been associated with the military?

And so we ended our second trip to Norfolk and in fact this chapter closes all the research that Tom and I did together. Time moved on and sadly Tom passed away in September, 2006; to this day I feel his loss. Still, it is my dearest wish to tell our story so I have included a final chapter in which I write about discoveries that I made after his passing that tie a lot of things together. Much of the information did come from psychic insights, which of course cannot be proven, although there are some thought-provoking matters arising from the historical research that will leave you wondering… it could be true.

8

The Ghost Woman

What a character was Mary Stringer, the femme fatale who allegedly brought strife upon the Townshends. There may not be any proof that she ever existed and the only surviving records that possibly relate to members of her family are held at Staffordshire, where I believe they resettled. There are also the parish records for Norfolk that may reference a daughter of hers. Mostly, I have to rely on the accounts that I gathered from channelling with spirit, so I'll continue with her story.

I believe her family were descended from the Stringers at Raynham. It seems that they were a family who had been in occupation at Raynham for generations, and that a branch of them settled at Castletownshend at some time during the late 1600s. The family that Mary came from was a second or third generation of these. Unfortunately her parents had social problems; I believe that her father Samuel was a drunkard and a ne'er-do-well who with his wife Mary lived off the auspices of the Poor Law in one place or another throughout their lives. Mental illness was an issue here, rooted in Samuel's upbringing, so one must not be too judgemental.

My information is that she was born circa 1732 at Castletownshend in Ireland, sometime in the month of April. Her Christian name comes from records in Staffordshire and Norfolk, which I believe relate to her, and it seems that her mother had the same name, which is more than mere coincidence. Mary was the eldest survivor of quite a few offspring. Brought up in poverty, she was accustomed to a harsh life and there were times when she had been starving. From reading about Irish social history for that period, it figures that this had been during the Irish Famine of 1740–1741. Times were very hard for the peasants during this period, although the gentry were comfortable enough.

From around the age of twelve she was employed as a domestic servant at the manor, where it's likely that she first became associated with George and Benjamin. It seems that from the outset of her employment she soon brought disgrace upon herself with her wayward behaviour, especially when, notoriously, she fell pregnant by George.

It transpired that he let her down concerning this with disastrous consequences, both for her and especially for the infant, whom I believe was a boy. However, in spite of what happened she still became his mistress later on from about the age of fourteen, living in a townhouse provided by him at Kinsale. During this relationship she bore him two or maybe three more children, who were daughters. She was comfortable enough here, living in accordance with George's wishes, although he insisted that she earned some of her own money as he didn't believe in spoiling her. It's coming through that she took in sewing and also that she had a talent for singing, dancing and playing musical instruments. She would have performed at the local taverns and hostelries so, generally speaking, it was a good life she had then.

Around the age of eighteen, I gather that she started getting ideas above her station and perhaps rivalry had a bearing on this, something to do with Charlotte Compton of whom she became exceedingly jealous as George was intent on marrying her at this time. This would have prompted Mary to insist on having her children bestowed with the same privileges as Benjamin Franklin.

It was her downfall as George found this unacceptable, so at length Mary was rejected and left with nothing except her children. He told her she would have to take them and rejoin her family who, as it happened, were soon to resettle in England. He must have been aware of this at some point. She was very distressed upon hearing this and tried to hang herself. But George thought it ridiculous that she should expect her children to become part of the nobility – especially as she'd only borne female offspring – so he callously cut her off completely, even from upkeep of the children. This seems rather harsh. Did he have any right to do that? Surely it must have been because he wanted to ensure that the way was clear for his marriage, and Charlotte must have insisted that he got Mary out of the way. It was just tough luck. Women in those days didn't have many rights, least of all those who were not lawfully wed. It was a chance she had taken and unfortunately she had come off worse in the long term.

Resettlement

In 1753, aged about twenty, Mary moved with her family to the West Midlands where they became settled in the locality of Great Wyrley in Staffordshire. This had probably been arranged by Resettlement Examination for the poor. Upon learning about such records while researching Mary Stringer, it felt significant that this was of relevance to her. That time in England was a period of great social and economic change. The growth of industry in the West Midlands led to a dramatic increase in population as people flocked to the urban areas for work and it is possible that the local authorities of the day, including Ireland being under the English Crown, farmed their poor to this area.

After extensive research in the Staffordshire records, I traced more relatives of the Samuel Stringer whom Tom and I had previously found a burial entry for in 1760. I found three baptisms of sons born to Samuel and Mary Stringer of Great Wyrley in the years of 1753, 1755 and 1761. It is interesting that the earliest date for the baptisms coincides with their alleged resettlement date and the last birth is just after the recorded death of Samuel. It also seems that the family moved away at some stage as there are no more burial records for them in this borough.

Mary found work as a serving wench at what was then a coaching inn, nowadays known as 'The Rising Sun' public house at Brownhills. In a short space of time, she and her daughters took lodgings there when she became the mistress of the innkeeper. This was the publican whom Liz had once alleged her former incarnation to be involved with. In all she stayed there for about two years.

During this time, I believe that George and Benjamin made occasional visits to the inn on their sojourns in the area. In one year, I think they made something like half a dozen visits, staying for a few days each time, so the three of them became re-acquainted. All appeared to be well, although I understand that this was when Mary began charging them for her favours.

Apparently, this was the start of a going concern for Mary and the innkeeper. Over the following months, the coaching inn became well known for the 'extra services' provided and of course the publican was a beneficiary of it. Ironically, it was at this time that she contracted venereal disease; I think it was syphilis.

It seems that Mary's mercenary traits knew no limits since it came through to me that from this time onwards she also hired out her eldest daughter, who was about seven years of age, to those who preferred young children. Considering the age of consent for a girl in those days, perhaps it was not thought to be quite such a bad thing.

Some time around then, Mary also became aware of Benjamin's rancour with George and they conspired to be rid of him, an idea that had appealed to Benjamin initially. Both were consumed with bitterness and resentment because of George's treatment of them. As I have said, Benjamin stood to gain a generous portion of George's estate upon him dying beforehand, probably by means of a special trust fund. However, the plans were dropped when Mary became too greedy concerning what she considered to be her rightful share, since she herself would have carried out the murder. To cover himself, Benjamin told George of her intentions, whereupon George took legal action against her and she was summoned to a court hearing at Lichfield, Staffordshire.

They escorted her to the courtroom, which was probably at the Guild Hall, riding on horseback from the coaching inn. On their way, they stopped off at the point where Liz had recollections of the scene that she referred to as her "betrayal by both of them". Seizing the moment, she tried to escape but was suppressed, just as Liz had said.

My intuition is that the trial was an open and shut case, concluded in all of two to three hours. I can't be sure how it went exactly, but I'm aware that the jury was sympathetic towards her. The offence was treated as a misdemeanour and she was sentenced to something like a month in gaol, while Benjamin received a fine for his part in it. Not the verdict George had wanted. Could this be why his father didn't include him in the draft wills that he made around this time? Again, my word has to be taken for these events, as I believe that George had the records of them removed from the Quarter Sessions at a later date. Mary's hatred towards them both grew even more thereafter and this was probably why Mary began blackmailing George after he murdered Benjamin.

She soon became dissatisfied with her lowly status at the coaching inn and began nagging the innkeeper for co-tenancy. Well she had made a substantial contribution to his revenue, after all. He refused her point blank so it can probably be imagined what she did next: she told the landlord what had been going on, of course. I believe that he was a member of the Arblaster family from Longdon; there is mention of them in the local history records. As it happened, the landlord took heed of her as he had already heard rumours of it. And as she anticipated, he was not impressed, clean-living man that I believe he was. The innkeeper was duly evicted, although Mary ensured that she had already left beforehand, as there would have been trouble otherwise.

So Mary disappeared into the woodwork, allegedly staying with family members at Great Wyrley and at Walsall Wood. It was probably at this point that the syphilis infection took hold of her and she became very ill. Her mother went to the local clergy who made arrangements to have Mary admitted to an infirmary-type institution, a quarantine house set aside for nursing cases of venereal disease. The term 'Foul Wards' comes to mind. Indeed, I learned that these sort of institutions had to deal with leprosy-type cases that other hospitals wouldn't touch. Situated in a back street of Walsall, this was a primitive place set up for the poor, more of a Bedlam-like house really. She was probably given mercury for her ailments there, as this was how such cases were treated in those days. I think she was discharged from there after about three months.

Mary probably could not get local employment thereafter because of the stigma attached to her illness and her bad reputation, which would have spread far around the local community 'like wildfire'. After a period of something like five months, I understand that she had to attend a few meetings with the Poor Law Administration, whereupon she was assessed along with a group of other 'undesirables' and in essence told that she would no longer be supported in that area.

There must have been numerous cases such as hers, since venereal disease reached epidemic proportions by the mid-eighteenth century. I'm not sure how the system worked, but I fathom that where possible the authorities farmed out such cases to the rural counties. It somehow rings a bell that this was a manoeuvre of local government in those days, done on a pretext of something else. Perhaps Mary told them that she had family connections in Norfolk and it was possible that she could start afresh there, or something to that effect anyway.

She was also probably told that the father of her daughters should be made responsible for their upkeep. According to research I did into this, there is an interesting piece of information relating to the legislation on 'Bastardy Bonds' from 1711–1752 that supports this rather well. When a woman did not marry, she and her offspring were liable to become a burden on the parish and so officials were anxious to trace the father. The woman would be questioned as to his identity and, once this was established, the father would be required to support his children; this was not unlike the work of the present Child Support Agency in the UK.

Thus by a twist of fate she was transferred – or perhaps 'ejected' would be more appropriate – to Raynham, Norfolk, to begin a new life. One might be inclined to think that justice had been served here since George really shouldn't have cut her off completely in the first place.

She was received well at Raynham by the Stringer family, as they were goodly people of a kind and compassionate nature. At some stage, doors were opened for her at a Townshend residence as a domestic servant; this was based somewhere in Norfolk, but it was probably not Raynham Hall. Wherever it was, the Viscountess Townshend was compassionate towards her too and wanted to help as she thought that her son had treated Mary and her little ones terribly. So Mary took employment with them for a while.

George was almost certainly away from Norfolk when this had taken place. When he did become aware of it, her presence was thought to be of little consequence – a nuisance, yes, but not a threat. Apparently, the reunion with his daughters also meant nothing to him, even though responsibility for them had been thrown back onto him. How he must have resented paying though and I'm sure it didn't go down well with his wife either.

In all, Mary lived in Norfolk in one place or another for something like a year. During this time, she became involved with a fisherman who was living at Holt and it transpired to be a significant liaison. They could have first met through a trading connection he had with the Townshends, he being the supplier of their fish. He was a low-life character, a lawless and rowdy hard drinker; in short, he was a reprobate who was involved with all manner of vices.

The fisherman enigma

There is definitely a connection here, and I now believe that the fisherman was in fact the father of 'Rickets', not the Third Viscount Townshend as I had been led to believe initially. Apparently, this had been an interruption by 'Rickets' while Charlotte and I had been discussing him during that rather eventful Christmas of 1997. Apparently, Ruth Barnes was his mother. I understand that his father had sired numerous offspring by different women in his time, perhaps not surprisingly, and that he was much older than Mary.

I don't think that they were from Norfolk but had resettled here to make a fresh start, possibly because of being up to no good previously. In connection with this, I recall 'Rickets' alleging once that his name had been Christopher Bath, although this is very dubious. This came from one of the many chilling encounters I had with him during my sleep, although occasionally there was some truth in what he conveyed. According to him, there was no chance of becoming prosperous in Norfolk in his era and actually, from what I've learned since about society in Georgian England, this sounds very likely so it doesn't surprise me that lawlessness was rife back then.

I'm of the belief that they lived at Holt, although this can't be proved. Certainly, there's no listing for this name in the Norfolk records, nor can any trading connection be made with Raynham Hall, not that one would expecting to find any. But in any case, it became clear to me that it was the father of 'Rickets' whom Tom had chanced to meet on that momentous visit to the fishermen's lair. It also seems clear that it was he who had been my mysterious attacker at Great Yarmouth. So what was all that about, one might ask? I believe his hostility towards me had a link with George's involvement with the smuggling: perhaps George had crossed him in a deal, resulting in a bit of a disagreement, shall we say. George lost two front teeth in this and he also lost the use of his legs because of a broken spine, I feel.

Subsequently, I think that both the father and the son came to sticky ends. In the case of 'Rickets', I'm aware that he was murdered by assassins hired by George and his body disposed of in a river; he was then found at some point, but the corpse had rotted beyond rec-ognition by then. I understand there was an enquiry made that tried to identify him even so, as he conveyed to me at one time that "The corpse was displayed like an exhibit in a museum." It seems that they concluded by writing him off as a missing person and I think his father met a similar end.

Returning to the thread of the story concerning Mary, it comes to me that something untoward took place concerning her daughters at this time, that they were sold on to a 'procurer of children' – it sounds incredible. In fact, I believe that the fisherman was the perpetrator here, not Mary, because he wanted them out of the way. This would seem to be quite in character. The deed was unknown to Mary when it took place and, although we don't know what the circumstances were exactly, she would have had no control of what happened. It is incred-ible to think that she stayed in a relationship with him thereafter, but apparently she did. Perhaps it was more of a business contact really: he supplied her with contraband goods, as north Norfolk was especially notorious for this at the time. On reflection, it appears that Mary was often the victim of abusive relationships in her lifetime although there were also times when she'd been an instigator.

When the Stringer family eventually discovered the deed, they rescued at least one or maybe two of the girls from this dreadful fate and adopted them as their own. I think that George had a part in helping out too, paying for their retrieval. So he did have some redeeming features after all. Did the fisherman get any punishment for his dastardly deed? Well yes, I believe that he was put in the stocks for a couple of days, during which he would have been pelted with all manner of foul things.

Supporting evidence

The time at which these events supposedly happened pre-dated official adoption papers. However, I traced shreds of evidence in the parish registers that suggest there could have been a girl by the name of Mary adopted by a Robert Stringer and his wife Mary, nee Playford, who lived at West Rudham. This is close to West Raynham as it happens and in fact they were relatives of the Stringers at West Raynham.

Robert was a seafaring man and records show that he was away at sea for a period of ten years. During this time there appears to be an added entry for a daughter named Mary, born the 15th of October, 1745. Looking closely at this, I suspect the register could have been altered since the entry does appear rather awkward in places. (Intriguingly, this date coincides with my account concerning Madam Sin's offspring by George.) Of course, it could be argued that Robert's wife gave birth to an illegitimate child during his absence; indeed, the entry is written as such when you know what to look for. Or did she in fact feign this for the record in order to protect the identity of the adopted child? I'll go with my instinct that tells me this record is a lie. In addition, it's possible that I've traced the marriage of this girl: there's an entry for a Mary Stringer who was wed to a Clement Fox at West Rudham on the 4th of July, 1763. If this is the same Mary, she would have been almost eighteen years old, a normal age for marriage. From further research I found that Clement was a fisherman originating from South Creake, and as it happens this was also where she was buried.

I believe that the Viscountess Townshend was very supportive of the girls and treated them like the grandchildren they really were, while for George's part there's evidence that he paid special attention to all his female offspring in his Last Will and Testament.

The scandal

So now we come to the fateful rumour that eventually led to Benjamin's murder. From what I gather, Mary uttered a few snipes against George and Benjamin while she was at Norfolk, most of which were dismissed as being sour grapes. The crunch came when Charlotte became pregnant with George's first child. This would have been sometime during 1754. Mary started a rumour that Benjamin was the father. I can see why Tom had said he was surprised that it was believed at all. Still, following this George ensured that she would cause no more trouble by seeing to it that she was drummed out of Norfolk.

So our malicious trouble-maker returned to Staffordshire under a cloud. To stand her in good stead she had the illicit earnings she had made while in the company of the fisherman; indeed, her reasons for staying with him start to become clearer now. She lived somewhere in the locality of Brownhills – Hammerwich comes to mind – and later she moved to Walsall, where I gather she made a comfortable living out of prostitution. She acquired a few regular clients who were well-to-do, some of whom, I believe, were noteworthy solicitors in the area. It appears that her bad reputation hadn't reached this far. Thus she continued for about three years until the turning point in the story.

Something like a year after her return, there was the momentous occasion when her mother gave her the news of a murder at Tamworth Castle, said to involve His Lordship and his half-brother. She had heard this from a friend who had been a serving maid there. The matter had been kept quiet, of course, and in fact, the maid had waited until she had left her employment before she mentioned anything. This would be why quite some time had passed before Mary came to hear of it. The maid happened to find the dead body of Benjamin in the castle dungeon around four a.m. one morning. Also, at the back gatehouse, she came upon a satchel belonging to him that contained his business documents, which she kept hold of. Moreover, she later spoke of an account from a mail man, who by chance had overheard the fight between George and Benjamin at the back gatehouse around noon of the day before. Condemning evidence, it appears.

After gathering this information, Mary conferred with her 'legal contacts', who were understandably interested in these findings. It was they who devised Mary's blackmail strategy, which lasted for a period of two years. In all, it took just two letters to George. The first he contested, as the maid in question would not testify, being naturally afraid. The second letter he could not dismiss. Apparently, it was the testimony of the mail man that gave the condemning evidence and George was advised by his own solicitor to agree to an out-of-court settlement; this would spare his neck, literally.

From communication received earlier, I'm aware that the figure of £12,000 was settled on. I suppose it has to be said that this was quite an achievement for someone who had a very limited education; a classic example of having contacts in high places.

I believe that Mary met with George at Timoleauge in Southern Ireland to get her payment, or at least one such as it's quite possible he may have paid in instalments. This was a discreet place that was far enough away from his home territory. She went over with her solicitor and took lodgings there, and the solicitor was upstairs when George made an appearance, listening to what went on as a witness. Upon handing over the money, George threatened to kill her if she continued blackmailing him but she was defiant to the last. She was aged about twenty-nine at the time of this momentous event.

Upon researching this, I found that in fact there was a prestigious firm of solicitors based at Walsall called Addison, Jesson and Copper that was connected to the High Court of England at the time these accounts allegedly happened. This may be a coincidence for there are certainly no surviving records of any such dealings I've mentioned.

What Mary did next

After an interlude of returning to Staffordshire to sort out some of her banking arrangements, Mary moved to Norfolk to be re-united with the fisherman. I'm sure this was partly to spite George – he had banished her from there but was now coerced into lifting the ban, a parliamentary minister having to give way to the likes of her. Never before had she wielded so much power and she would have loved it. She bought a large house at Caister-on-Sea, which was an up-market location in those days, where she and her partner resided. He continued as a fisherman, however, as he loved the sea and the income he gained from his various dealings paid for their lifestyle.

At some point, Mary gave support to her daughters and wanted to be re-united with them as she regretted what had gone before. I think she had her wish, although it's unlikely that one can go so far as to say that she was loved by them since the rift was too wide and they would never have been able to trust her completely again, nor the company she kept. Indeed, their mother was an evil woman.

Mary's controlling side emerged now, apparently especially relating to the fisherman's ineptitude with money since he was often in debt. He grew to resent what he regarded as her hen-pecking concerning this and a rift developed between them. He was not the sort to be pushed around by a woman. She even infringed on the acquisitions made from his illicit dealings and moved in one day, quite unexpectedly, while he was at a smuggling site, 'poking her nose in'. This was Liz's recollection of Madam Sin walking along the beach to see what her partner had acquired.

He reacted to her overbearing ways by keeping the company of other mistresses and in return she took to brothel-keeping with a view to becoming a famous Madam of her time. For about four years in all she ran two such enterprises, one in Caister and the other in London, thus becoming even more wealthy, although she'd sold her soul for it. I recall that Liz had once said that she thought the practice was somewhere in London so it seems she was half right anyway.

I believe that Mary had become pregnant, perhaps by the fisherman, around this time although the baby was stillborn. Soon after the birth, I think she buried it somewhere – a beach comes to mind. The fisherman was left out of all this and actually I don't think he knew what she'd done at first. He already felt a great deal of resentment towards her by then in any case and this only made things worse. In return, he poisoned her by contaminating her food. One day, he stirred some dirty water into a pot of gravy stored in the larder, unknown to the cook. Mary caught consumption from it and she died slowly and painfully, just as Tom had said. She was in her early forties by then.

Although there's no burial record for her, it was my and Tom's thought that she was buried at Great Yarmouth, possibly in an unmarked grave, a pauper's burial site or something like that. The local council told us of a cemetery where there is a likely site for such a burial ground, although upon visiting it we couldn't tune in to the exact spot. Intriguingly, though, the general place did have a familiar energy for us. Since then I have come to believe that this place is connected with her partner's grave and that Mary herself was buried on a beach; this seems likely and it does tally with my earlier insight about an unmarked grave. Whatever the case, just like Benjamin Franklin, she is indeed lost in the sands of time.

Having related this story of Mary's life, I find many of her actions detestable and some of them quite unbelievable. However, I feel sure that what I've understood is correct and this is the clearest account I can give.

Benjamin's murder

A rift had developed between George and Benjamin around this time and relations had deteriorated to such a pitch that they no longer spoke. Quite possibly the episode at the courtroom in Lichfield had a bearing on this. George was staying at Tamworth Castle while Benjamin had ridden on horseback from Leek; I think George had relayed a message to Benjamin that he wanted to see him, or something like this. Certainly Benjamin felt daunted about having to fit it in with his plans, although he wanted to resolve the issue once and for all.

He'd been staying with a friend who was connected with commerce, a banker perhaps. My feeling is that there was frequent contact between these two because there was some business that Benjamin had at Stoke that was of significance, something to do with politics. I have an insight that he was an MP for that area, appointed by Earl Granville, and was at the beginning of what could have been a promising career in politics. Indeed, nothing could have been further from his interests than this meeting with George.

I couldn't trace any tangible evidence of this, although I'll mention that Tom and I had always felt an important energy with certain places on the outskirts of Stoke on Trent, those around Trentham and Leek especially.

Upon his arrival sometime around noon, George met with him outside and took him to the back gatehouse since this was as out of the way as possible. It appears that he must have been anticipating a fight for it seems there were no servants around at the time, which is strange. Perhaps George had ensured that they were all absent when he arranged this meeting as he didn't want witnesses. This would have been because of the untoward nature of the issues he wanted to have out. He was hostile from the outset. "I hear you've been fraternizing with my wife…" Thus the scene developed as Tom had conveyed. Ironically, I believe that Benjamin would have lived had he not retaliated.

George was devastated by his actions as he hadn't intended to kill Benjamin. In the heat of the moment, he lost control. Then in a panic, he bound up Benjamin's hands and feet and took him to the dungeon where he left him until the following day where he was discovered by a maid servant in the early hours of the following morning. She had returned unexpectedly as there was something she had forgotten and whatever it was made her feel somewhat embarrassed, so she crept in at this time hoping to be unnoticed. My sense is that she went to the back gatehouse first of all, where she found the satchel. Upon then going to the courtyard, I see her noticing a trail of blood leading to the dungeon. She followed this and upon looking in she saw Benjamin's corpse chained to the wall. She quickly stole away, taking the satchel with her. So much for the precautions George had taken beforehand.

Later that day he put the corpse in a sack and rode with it to Milford, which is quite a distance away. He would have chosen Oat Hill for the burial because it had significance in treasured memories; I think they had spent many a happy hour playing there in their childhood years. There were some connections they had around Stafford I feel, possibly with the Ansons at Shugborough Hall, but this is uncertain. On a more practical note, perhaps that this was a remote spot situated on high ground had a bearing on it because I know for a fact that Cannock Chase was liable to flooding in those days and was well-known for being treacherous when that happened. In any case this event was indeed a harrowing one and a most tragic time in George's life. After covering the body over, perhaps he said a prayer asking for forgiveness. Thereafter I believe that he went to get drunk, but this was not in celebration as Tom had once thought. On reflection it seems that George's life was a rollercoaster of sensational highs and abysmal lows, as far as I'm aware anyway.

Ruth Barnes

Since I have given an account of Mary Stringer, I feel that I should also include what else I know about Ruth. Again, much of this cannot be proved by anything tangible and her early life is a mystery. But I shall give you the story as I gather it.

This character has a few things in common with Mary, although I don't think she had quite the sleazy life that Mary had, to be honest. Nor was her upbringing anything like as harsh. I gather that she was also of Irish origin, from the outskirts of Dublin. Her father was a merchant of some sort and they moved to London when Ruth was a girl. Here he had some trade link with the Townshends, whereupon Ruth got employment as a housemaid at one of their residences. She was around fifteen years of age by then and it was during her service there that I believe she took the eye of the Third Viscount.

Upon becoming pregnant by Charles, she returned to Dublin to give birth to the child whom I believe to have been Benjamin Franklin. It can't be proven, but I think Franklin was his maternal grandmother's maiden name. Indeed, there are scores of Franklins listed in Dublin for that era. I also see a link to Dublin with the gold cross pendant that Tom envisaged at Arleston Inn. The woman who gave it was from a wealthy family connected to a Catholic church; there's some association to the Third Viscount, I feel, or maybe to John Carteret.

Looking through the parish registers for Dublin, I found a possible entry under the name Barnes in the baptisms at St Catherine's, near the city centre. This does seem rather encouraging: there is a Ruth Barnes born on the 18th of December, 1711, to a Samuel and Ann Barnes. Also it appears that she had an elder sister and a younger brother born in the years of 1710 and 1713 respectively. There are no other entries for this family in Dublin, nor for the whole of Ireland even, so perhaps they moved away as I have suggested.

Finally, the enemy is unmasked

"I know that when the stress has grown too strong Thou will be there.
I know that when the waiting seems so long, Thou hearest prayer.
I know that through the crash of falling worlds Thou holdest me.
I know that life and death are all Thine eternally."

Since this story hinges upon dreams, it's fitting that I should end with one. The theme does tie things up rather well. There was a vivid dream that I had one bleak morning in January, 1995. On reflection, I'm also aware of similar dream encounters prior to meeting Tom, although they were not quite as vivid but had that same element of menace about them even so. It made me realise that indeed there was a reason why I had to meet him at that specific time in my life, so that I could evade the pitfalls that were being lain by evil spirits. It's true that this had started since my childhood, as I remember, and that these machinations had been coming to a head rather dangerously.

The scene began in a very ordinary setting. I was aware of being at secondary school during a dinner break, of taking a tray from the trolley in the canteen and counting my money to see how I could spend it. Very similar in fact to what I used to do at the time of this dream. I was living at Telford near the town centre and it was my habit to go for a lunch break at the canteen in a local supermarket. It seems like my past and what was then my present were meeting up here.

In the dream, I was aware of others congregating in the dinner hall when suddenly music started playing and we were all affected by some kind of power that numbed us. Over time this increased until a person was taken over. It was something we were accustomed to though, and some unknown alien power was causing it. It was not just here either but everywhere, and there was nothing to stop it. I became aware that a friend I knew from college had joined the dinner queue just then. I recognised Fran's short stature and long red hair, which were her distinguishing features as were also the blue denim jeans and jacket that she often used to wear. We didn't speak but I knew that she was aware of me too.

From there I found myself on the playing fields at my primary school. The scene was Sports Day and there were rows of chairs set out on the grass, arranged in the familiar layout of such events, placed facing each other with a gangway running up the middle. I was sitting alone, but there were other children present. Every so often, I noticed my friend. Sometimes she was sitting next to me, at others times she was sitting on the row opposite, talking with others. I saw her glance my way every so often, as if she were keeping an eye on me.

Suddenly the music started again, stronger than ever, and I felt the left side of my body becoming totally numb. Something within me stirred, telling me to sing a song that was of my own choosing. My voice rose above the music and on so doing the other children joined in, singing songs of their own choice also. The force lost its power and retreated. Strangely, though, this seems to have been taken for granted by everyone and they resumed normality as if nothing had happened – everyone, that is, except for my friend who was aware of what I'd done. She sat alone this time and continued watching me from the opposite side.

I left my seat and walked towards another one. This time it was in a park, which I recognised to be the one at Telford town centre.

It seems like I was doing a fair bit of time travelling in this dream! Curiously, I was followed by my friend who came and sat next to me to my left, looking at me intently as though she wanted to talk. The conversation was telepathic. She looked directly into my eyes and told me that she had seen me thwart the power of the music on the playing field. But she expressed it in such a way that I should feel guilty about it: "Why, you're on our side, aren't you?" This is what she seemed to say, looking at me deeply and searchingly as if she were playing some kind of mind game.

I told her that I didn't want to speak with her, as I began to doubt that she was what she appeared to be. I left my seat in the alcove and proceeded onto a paved incline, which I recognised to be the town shopping centre, not far from the town park in fact. She remained seated and watched me walk away and I was pleased to gain some distance from her. However, upon looking back I saw her following in the distance. I continued forward and the next thing I knew was that, incredibly, she had gained ground on me. There she was, stalking in from the left-hand side. The next thing I knew was that she was up ahead, unfortunately.

We came upon a contemporary art sculpture set in the paved area. She moved to the opposite side of it and I looked at her through a gap from my side. We seemed to talk to each other with this barrier between us, then suddenly she came over to my side and produced a penknife. I recognised this as being one I had when I was a teenager. I knew it was very blunt, more of an ornament really, but even so she attacked me with it, stabbing the point onto my forehead; strangely, it bounced off. I took the knife from her and did likewise to her, though the effect was the same. This bizarre fight carried on for a while as we kept handing the knife back and forth to each other, taking turns to stab at each other's foreheads. How weird!

During this quarrel – as I believe that's what it was – someone whom I knew from a training course at Telford passed by. He was the only other person about and I approached him imploring for help. It was no good as I found that he was unable to see my attacker since she was invisible to him. So he continued along his way, ignoring me, as if

I weren't right in the head. I turned to her once more and she looked back at me defiantly, as if to say, "You know how it is now. They won't help you!" She then seized my left arm and produced a razor blade, whereupon she cut a deep circle around the vein – the one used when I go to my GP for blood tests. Her intention was to gouge a lump out of it, but I pulled away before she got that far. I felt no pain but the attack had turned vicious, especially as I'm aware of the significance. She went on to inflict several small nicks to my arms with this blade.

I retreated behind the sculpture and began retaliating, except that this time it was verbal. Strangely, I could see my jibes being absorbed by a tunnel of white light that came between us. I only had a vague awareness of this but I knew it was there as some kind of mitigating energy force. I don't know what I said but in one instance it must have been close to the bone, as what appeared to be a young woman ominously warned me to take care or else I would see what I was really contending with.

The last impressions I recall clearly were of the paved incline meeting the skyline and that thing that I thought to be Fran obscuring my way. It's difficult to describe, but I vaguely saw what looked like the figure of a man, or an alien, which faded into a dark silhouette. I then awoke with the feeling I would have seen something terrible if things had continued. Perhaps this was an implication that my attacker could still cause damage in the future, given half a chance, despite the recent defeat. They just don't give up.

A call to spiritual awakening

"I will pour out my spirit on all flesh; your sons and daughters
shall prophesy, your old men shall dream dreams,
and your young men shall see visions."

– JOEL 2:28

Coming back to 2015 now, no doubt many readers will see links to the New World Order here, considering the insidious power exerted by the music that I now realise alluded to 'mind control'. That it was a takeover ploy by 'an alien power' especially suggests this. I didn't know anything about such things back then; it wasn't widely known about. Nowadays it's more a question of who hasn't heard of organisations such as the Illuminati?

Or perhaps this is all mere coincidence? After all, everyone knows that dreams don't mean anything, do they? Forget it. But I can't…

I am no longer menaced by that evil spirit who I know to have been 'Rickets'. He was my worst enemy by far. Whether or not some readers can accept this, I'll mention that he was extinguished a few years ago and no longer exists. In fact, I glimpsed him when he was dying, early one morning in June, 2010. The ultimate death, I believe. A controversial statement, I know, but I believe there can be a weeding out of souls. And so I'll end my book by saying that he will not be back. Nevertheless, life unfolds further and there will be yet more secrets waiting to be uncovered.

Shalom

If you have enjoyed this book ...

Local Legend is committed to publishing the very best spiritual writing, both fiction and non-fiction. You might also enjoy:

DAY TRIPS TO HEAVEN

T J Hobbs (ISBN 978-1-907203-99-2)

The author's debut novel is a brilliant description of life in the spiritual worlds and of the guidance available to all of us on Earth as we struggle to be the best we can. Ethan is learning to be a guide but having a hard time of it, with too many questions and too much self-doubt. But he has potential, so is given a special dispensation to bring a few deserving souls for a preview of the afterlife, to help them with crucial decisions they have to make in their lives. The book is full of gentle humour, compassion and spiritual knowledge, and it asks important questions of us all.

A UNIVERSAL GUIDE TO HAPPINESS

Joanne Gregory (ISBN 978-1-910027-06-6)

Joanne is an internationally acclaimed clairaudient medium with a celebrity contact list. Growing up, she ignored her evident psychic abilities, fearful of standing out from others, and even later, despite witnessing miracles daily, her life was difficult. But then she began to learn the difference between the psychic and the spiritual, and her life turned round.

This is her spiritual reference handbook – a guide to living happily and successfully in harmony with the energy that created our universe. It is the knowledge and wisdom distilled from a lifetime's experience of working with spirit.

THE QUIRKY MEDIUM
Alison Wynne-Ryder (ISBN 978-1-907203-47-3)

Alison is the co-host of the TV show *Rescue Mediums*, in which she puts herself in real danger to free homes of lost and often malicious spirits. Yet she is a most reluctant medium, afraid of ghosts! This is her amazing and often very funny autobiography, taking us 'back stage' of the television production as well as describing how she came to discover the psychic gifts that have brought her an international following.

Winner of the Silver Medal in the national Wishing Shelf Book Awards.

SIMPLY SPIRITUAL
Jacqui Rogers (ISBN 978-1-907203-75-6)

The 'spookies' started contacting Jacqui when she was a child and never gave up until, at last, she developed her psychic talents and became the successful international medium she is now. This is a powerful and moving account of her difficult life and her triumph over adversity, with many great stories of her spiritual readings. The book was a Finalist in The People's Book Prize national awards.

AURA CHILD
A I Kaymen (ISBN 978-1-907203-71-8)

One of the most astonishing books ever written, telling the true story of a genuine Indigo child. Genevieve grew up in a normal London family but from an early age realised that she had very special spiritual and psychic gifts. She saw the energy fields around living things, read people's thoughts and even found herself slipping through time, able to converse with the spirits of those who had lived in her neighbourhood. This is an uplifting and inspiring book for what it tells us about the nature of our minds.

5P1R1T R3V3L4T10N5

Nigel Peace (ISBN 978-1-907203-14-5)

With descriptions of more than a hundred proven prophetic dreams and many more everyday synchronicities, the author shows us that, without doubt, we can know the future and that everyone can receive genuine spiritual guidance for our lives' challenges. World-renowned biologist Dr Rupert Sheldrake has endorsed this book as "…vivid and fascinating… pioneering research…" and it was national runner-up in The People's Book Prize awards.

CELESTIAL AMBULANCE

Ann Matkins (ISBN 978-1-907203-45-9)

A brave and delightful comedy novel. Having died of cancer, Ben wakes up in the afterlife looking forward to a good rest, only to find that everyone is expected to get a job! He becomes the driver of an ambulance (with a mind of her own), rescuing the spirits of others who have died suddenly and delivering them safely home. This book is as thought-provoking as it is entertaining.

TAP ONCE FOR YES

Jacquie Parton (ISBN 978-1-907203-62-6)

This extraordinary book offers powerful evidence of human survival after death. When Jacquie's son Andrew suddenly committed suicide, she was devastated. But she was determined to find out whether his spirit lived on, and began to receive incredible yet undeniable messages from him… Several others also then described deliberate attempts at spirit contact. This is a story of astonishing love and courage, as Jacquie fought her own grief and others' doubts in order to prove to the world that her son still lives.

These titles are all available as paperbacks and eBooks. Further details and extracts of these and many other beautiful books may be seen at

www.local-legend.co.uk

Lightning Source UK Ltd.
Milton Keynes UK
UKOW06f1136040216

267728UK00008B/169/P

9 781910 027134